"I maintain that disciples of Jesus Christ are obligated to adhere to the theological consensus of the church; that is, its beliefs that are firmly rooted in Scripture have passed the test of time in terms of their orthodoxy and provide critical guardrails for its existence and practice. The Nicene Creed is a primary example of theological consensus, and its exposition by Coleman Ford and Shawn Wilhite serves Jesus's disciples very well. This clearly written, well-structured, nicely illustrated, and thoroughly researched book covers the essential biblical, theological, historical, and practical elements of this venerable creed."

—**Gregg R. Allison**, professor of Christian theology, The Southern Baptist Theological Seminary

"*Nicaea for Today* offers a compelling vision for the Nicene Creed's enduring relevance. As the authors convey with clarity and warmth the beauty of this ancient confession, they invite evangelicals into a more rooted theological, spiritual, and missional life. For those seeking to deepen their understanding of trinitarian theology and its transformative vibrance today, or for those asking how to convey this to others, this book is a perfect choice."

—**Megan DeVore**, professor of church history and early Christian studies, Colorado Christian University

"I heartily applaud the efforts of Coleman Ford and Shawn Wilhite to provide readers with this outstanding exploration of the historical context, key participants, theological commitments, and biblical considerations related to the Nicene Creed. In helping readers 'think Nicenely,' our authors, on the occasion of the 1700th anniversary of the Council of Nicaea, have given us a thoughtful and pro-Nicene exposition of the creed, advocating for its adoption in private and public use. Ford and Wilhite offer insightful and pastoral guidance regarding the role of the creed at times of baptism and the Lord's Supper, in catechetical instruction, and in public worship, doing so with particular sensitivity to those in the free-church tradition. Pastors, church leaders, and students will benefit greatly from engaging this superb work."

—**David S. Dockery**, president and distinguished professor of theology, Southwestern Baptist Theological Seminary

"Ford and Wilhite offer a brief but thorough book. This work is accessible even to theological beginners, but it doesn't shy away from technical terms. The authors help readers grasp the story and essence of the biblical and doctrinal deliberations that produced this critical confessional statement. The Nicene Creed expresses biblical truths that the church must affirm and reaffirm in each new generation, and the authors of *Nicaea for Today* are certainly adroit guides in affirming these truths for today's church."

—**Stefana Dan Laing**, associate professor of divinity, Samford University Beeson Divinity School

"Too often, academic books speak above the heads of laypeople or beneath the discourse of experts. Not so with this one! It represents a perfect blend of scholarly erudition and ecclesial relevance. Ford and Wilhite mine the theological ore of the Nicene Creed, then offer its golden riches—purged of unnecessary rubble—to students, pastors, and thoughtful Christians in terms anyone can understand. The authors reveal that the Nicene Creed isn't some irrelevant parchment from history, but a living document that reverberates with divine energy for the twenty-first century. May we never forget that Nicaea is for today!"

—**Bryan M. Litfin**, professor of Bible and theology, Rawlings School of Divinity at Liberty University

"The Nicene Creed has been the Christian church's norming theology statement since the fourth century—quietly doing its job—often with little attention paid to it. Now, in this anniversary year, it takes the spotlight, and *Nicaea for Today* shows not only its historical importance but its ongoing relevance in the life of the church. Ford and Wilhite do an excellent job of telling its story, drawing out the creed's implications in the life of the Christian believer. Theology matters, and this book tells you why."

—**Greg Peters**, professor of medieval and spiritual theology, Biola University

"Ford and Wilhite offer a clear and helpful exposition of Nicene theology, but they also go further, showing how one might think in Nicene categories today. They write with pastoral warmth and eyes fixed firmly on church ministry concerns. This book will benefit academics and practitioners. It will enrich contemporary theological discussions and ministry practice."

—**David M. Rathel**, assistant professor of Christian theology, Gateway Seminary

"Study of the Nicene Creeds is a welcome trend by which many Christians today have been reinvigorated, and unfortunately, there have been few serious attempts at explaining its importance by those who know the history, theology, and literature well. Thankfully, experts like Ford and Wilhite took up the challenge! *Nicaea for Today* remarkably holds two things in balance: first, a deep, learned understanding of the Nicene Creed and its context, and second, an accessible demonstration of why it is important for today. The result is a book that is an absolute gift to the church."

—**Brandon D. Smith**, Chair of the Hobbs School of Theology and Ministry and associate professor of theology and early Christianity, Oklahoma Baptist University

"Seventeen hundred years after 'the Great and Holy Synod' that produced its first iteration, the Nicene Creed remains the touchpoint for any orthodox reading of Holy Scripture and its central message. Coleman Ford and Shawn Wilhite have produced an introduction to the creed's main themes that is both astute and accessible, both erudite and edifying. Their treatment is biblically grounded, historically careful, theologically informed, and practically relevant. This book will help its readers think 'Nicenely' about the glorious triune God and his life-changing gospel."

—**R. Lucas Stamps**, professor of Christian theology, Anderson University

"*Nicaea for Today* is that unique book that is not only highly readable and deeply engaging but also incredibly significant. As numerous polls constantly remind us, the greatest crisis that American evangelicals face today concerns the recovery of theological orthodoxy in churches and among Christian institutions. We should be thankful to the one Lord God, who is the Father and the Son and the Holy Spirit, that he called Shawn Wilhite and Coleman Ford to write this phenomenal text. Please take it, read it, and grow with it!"

—**Malcolm B. Yarnell III**, research professor of theology, Southwestern Baptist Theological Seminary

NICAEA for TODAY

NICAEA for TODAY

WHY AN ANCIENT CREED (STILL) MATTERS

COLEMAN M. FORD
SHAWN J. WILHITE

B&H
ACADEMIC®
BRENTWOOD, TENNESSEE

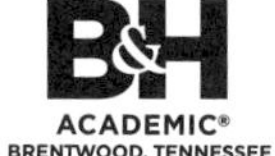

Nicaea for Today: Why an Ancient Creed (Still) Matters

Published by B&H Academic®
Brentwood, Tennessee

ISBN: 978-1-4300-9154-7

Dewey Decimal Classification: 238
Subject Heading: NICENE CREED \ JESUS
CHRIST \ DOCTRINAL THEOLOGY

Cover design by Gearbox. Front cover images: Basil II, surnamed the Bulgar-slayer (958–1025). Byzantine emperor (976–1025) from de Macedonian Dynasty. Detail from the Menologion of Basil II, Bridgeman Images; First Council of Nicaea (325), holding the Nicene-Constantinopolitan Creed of 381, Public Domain; First Council of Nicaea by Michael Damaskinos, Public Domain.

Printed in the United States of America

30 29 28 27 26 25 VP 1 2 3 4 5 6 7 8 9 10

To Colette, Matthieu, and Charlotte (aka "the Fordlings"):
that you may love and cherish the Savior who
was made flesh for your salvation.

—Coleman

To Mercy and Caden:
with hopeful prayers that you embrace the triune
God as envisioned by the Fathers of our faith.

—Shawn

CONTENTS

PREFACE

This is now the second book we have written together as friends and mutual lovers of Scripture, church history, and theology. Academic writing is a life we have pursued together. We are better together! Several years ago, while walking the halls of Southern Seminary and completing our doctoral work there, we certainly dreamt of writing books together. Now, we more enjoy the slower life, enjoyed over good coffee and conversations about music, theology, and things of the soul.

In our first book, we envisioned a model of pastoral ministry attuned to a slower practice and the contemplation of God for a more fruitful care of souls.[1] In *Nicaea for Today*, we seek to envision a theological model tethered to the Nicene Creed, the pro-Nicene traditions, and the theological disputes of the early church fathers as "sites" of theological memory.[2] The Nicene Creed is necessary

[1] Coleman M. Ford and Shawn J. Wilhite, *Ancient Wisdom for the Care of Souls: Learning the Art of Pastoral Ministry from the Church Fathers* (Crossway, 2024).

[2] Lewis Ayres, "Of Slowness and Distance: Reflections on Philology and the Curation of Tradition in Catholic Theology," in *New Narratives for Old: The Historical Method of Reading Early Christian Theology, Essays in Honor of Michel René Barnes*, ed. Anthony A. Briggman and Ellen Scully, CUA Studies in Early Christianity (Catholic University of America Press, 2022), 27–44.

for our theological fidelity and spiritual enrichment. Thus, our two books can be read together: a model of *pastoral ministry* from the Fathers and a model of *theology* from the Fathers, both written with a keen eye for the people in the pews and the newer students in the classroom.

As we envision it, so much of the art of writing involves self-discovery and is shaped by caring for those in our immediate ministry circles. Several early church fathers wrote books for small groups of people, and we are drawn to that kind of vision. Knowing that we set out to explore Nicene and pro-Nicene theology as an exercise in unpacking our own theological convictions, we hope to assist others along the way. We considered several questions, including these:

- What theological ideas are necessary for a Nicene vision?
- What theological and spiritual vision do we want to provide our children and those whom we love?
- While in the church and the classroom, what do we want the people we pastor and the students we teach to know about the era and culture of pro-Nicene theology?

Many people have invested in us and in this project. We have been shaped by these relationships, conversations, and mentors (both known and unknown). While we can never adequately express our thanks to everyone who has made this book possible, we will nevertheless make an attempt.

I (Coleman) wish to thank the administration and fellow colleagues at Southwestern Baptist Theological Seminary for their ongoing support of thoughtful scholarship for the church. Thank you to David Dockery, who has consistently encouraged and supported me. Many thanks also to colleagues Blake McKinney, Madison Grace, Malcolm Yarnell, and Trey Moss for their notes, feedback, and general encouragement during this project. I also wish to thank the pastors and ministry staff at The Village Church Denton, who allowed me to work alongside them while encouraging me to write and pursue my academic ministry. Finally, thank you to my wife, Alex, and to the Fordlings—Colette, Matthieu, and Charlotte—for the love, support, encouragement, cuddles, high fives, and hugs along the way.

I (Shawn) express my profound gratitude to my personal mentors and fellow colleagues and administrators at California Baptist University and Gateway Seminary. Chris Morgan and Tony Chute continue to encourage and support me in the service of the church. Many thanks are due to Trey Moss, Brian Davidson, David Rathel, Emmanuel Siordia, Conner Smith, and Luke Stamps. I wish to also thank a small group of people at Redeemer Baptist Church (especially Jessica Daily) who read portions of this book and forced me to clarify and simplify the Nicene ideas; they have an insatiable appetite for good theology! Lastly, to my wife, Allyson (who gave us the term *nicenely*), and my kiddies, Mercy and Caden: You are the delights of my soul! Thank you for our Star Wars and Harry Potter marathons, your love and care, and for simply being you!

Both of us are grateful to the editorial team at B&H Academic for stewarding this work. To Madison Trammel, Logan Pyron, and Michael McEwen: You have been an encouragement to us, and this project is better because of your work.

Coleman M. Ford and Shawn J. Wilhite
On the Feast Day of Matthew the Apostle
September 21, 2024

FOREWORD

It was during the fall of 1975 that I first read an entire work from the ancient church. It was Novatian's *De trinitate*. My systematic theology professor at the seminary where I was studying—Wycliffe College, an evangelical Anglican seminary at the University of Toronto—was Jakób Jocz (1906–1983), a remarkable Jewish Christian theologian and Anglican minister from Lithuania. Fluent in at least half a dozen languages, Jocz was an exacting teacher who was also gifted with a deep sense of the transcendent reality of the triune God. One often left Jocz's classes with a sense that one had been in the very presence of God as Jocz taught.

When Professor Jocz learned that I had done an undergraduate degree in philosophy, he told me that my assigned paper for his theology course in autumn 1975 was to be on Novatian on the Trinity. He did not ask me if I wanted to write on that subject. He simply stated, "Mr. Haykin, you will write on Novatian on the Trinity." I suspect that it was this essay that first kindled in my life a deep and abiding interest in the triunity of God that has never left me. And while it was the third-century Latin-speaking schismatic Novatian who kindled it, indirectly this interest is also a fruit of the teaching ministry of Professor Jocz.

It has been said that the rediscovery of the doctrine of the Trinity among Protestants and evangelicals in the latter decades of the twentieth century owes much to the writings of the Swiss theologian Karl Barth (1886–1968). During my formative years at Wycliffe College, I read next to nothing of Barth, although it became apparent during the years that I sat under Professor Jocz that Barth was a key theological influence on his thinking. So, possibly in a roundabout way, and that through Professor Jocz, Barth's trinitarianism influenced my fascination with this most fundamental of Christian doctrines. If so, that influence was quite beyond my horizon. Rather, it was the combination of the sense of the transcendent in Professor Jocz's teaching and an ancient church author, Novatian—the first theologian in Rome to write in Latin—who kindled a trinitarian flame that I hope will never be extinguished.

It is my prayer that the reading of this work on Nicene trinitarianism by two dear friends will have the very same effect on you, dear reader, and that a passion will be kindled such that your life and thinking will ever be for the glory of the consubstantial Trinity.

Michael A. G. Azad Haykin
Professor of church history and biblical spirituality
The Southern Baptist Theological Seminary
Louisville, KY

THE NICENE CREED (325)

We believe in one God, the Father Almighty, Maker of all things both visible and invisible.

[We believe] in one Lord, Jesus Christ, the Son of God, begotten from the Father, the only begotten—that is, from the substance (οὐσίας) of the Father, God from God, Light from Light, true God from true God, begotten, not made, *consubstantial* (ὁμοούσιον) with the Father, "through whom all things came to be" (John 1:3), both the things in heaven and the things on earth. For us humans and for our salvation, he descended and became incarnate. [He] became human, suffered, and rose on the third day. [He] ascended into the heavens and is coming "to judge the living and the dead" (2 Tim 4:1; 1 Pet 4:5).

And, [we believe] in the Holy Spirit.

But, as for those who say, "There was a time when he was not," and "before he was begotten, he was not," and that he came to be from nothing, or from a different *hypostasis* (ὑποστάσεως) or substance (οὐσίας), [who] claim that the Son of God is either [created or] mutable or alterable—The catholic and apostolic church anathematizes these people![1]

[1] Translation of § 135.c The Council of Nicaea (AD 325) translated by Shawn J. Wilhite. Critical Greek text and translation provided in Wolfram Kinzig, ed., *Faith in Formulae: A Collection of Early Christian Creeds and Creed-Related Texts*, Oxford Early Christian Texts (Oxford University Press, 2017), 290. See also Mark DelCogliano, "Creed of the Council of Nicaea (325)," in *God*, ed. Andrew Radde-Gallwitz, vol. 1, The Cambridge Edition of Early Christian Writings (Cambridge University Press, 2017), 114–15.

THE NICENO-CONSTANTINOPLE CREED (381)

We believe in one God, the Father, Almighty, Maker of heaven and earth and of all things both visible and invisible.

[We believe] in one Lord, Jesus Christ, the Son of God, the only begotten, who was begotten from the Father before all ages, Light from Light, true God from true God, begotten, not made, *consubstantial* (ὁμοούσιον) with the Father, "through whom all things came to be" (John 1:3). For us humans and for our salvation, he descended from the heavens and became incarnate from the Holy Spirit and the Virgin Mary, and [he] became human. For us, he was crucified under Pontius Pilate, suffered, was buried, and rose on the third day according to the Scriptures. [He] ascended into the heavens, is seated at the right hand of the Father, and is coming again with glory "to judge the living and the dead" (2 Tim 4:1; 1 Pet 4:5), whose kingdom will have no end.

[We believe] in the Holy Spirit, the Lord and giver of life, who proceeds from the Father [and the Son], who is worshipped and glorified together with the Father and the Son, [and] who has spoken through the prophets.

[We believe] in one, holy, catholic, and apostolic church.

We confess one baptism for the forgiveness of sins.

We await the resurrection of the dead and the life of the coming age. Amen.[1]

[1] Translation of § 184.e1 The Creed of Constantinople (Nicene-Constantinopolitan Creed, AD 381) translated by Shawn J. Wilhite. Critical Greek text provided in Wolfram Kinzig, *Faith in Formulae: A Collection of Early Christian Creeds and Creed-Related Texts,* Oxford Early Christian Texts (Oxford University Press, 2017), 511–12. See also Mark DelCogliano, "Creed of the Council of Constantinople (381)," in *God*, ed. Andrew Radde-Gallwitz, vol. 1, The Cambridge Edition of Early Christian Writings (Cambridge University Press, 2017), 268–69.

INTRODUCTION: THEOLOGIANS AS DOCTORS OF SACRED THINGS

The song "Theologians" by Chicago-based band Wilco, found on their 2004 album *A Ghost Is Born*, contains a line that has haunted us for years. In so many words, the vocalist contends that theologians know absolutely nothing about his soul.[1] As Christian theologians, our instinct is to say, "Now, hold on! We have been trained in the things of the soul!" Our desire has been to embody the classical notion of theologians as "doctors of the soul." We have a few degrees on the wall and scars on our hearts to prove it.

Certainly, we do not know the deep complexities of lead vocalist Jeff Tweedy's soul, or even of our own souls. However, we are fundamentally resolved that theologians *ought* to know something about the human soul and the life of God, as both "doctors of the soul" and "doctors of sacred things." The theologians of the church's early centuries knew quite a bit about the human soul. Theology was a *soulish* endeavor, and one mark of a good theologian was

[1] See Wilco, "Theologians," by Jeff Tweedy, Mikael Jorgensen, Chris Girard, track 10 on CD 1 of *A Ghost Is Born*, Nonesuch, 2004, compact disc.

a spiritual life marked by contemplation and attention to virtue.[2] Early Christian theologians were motivated to contend for humanity's souls amid constructive and critical theological assertions. In the early fourth century, knowing something about the soul led some theologians in the early church to gather in the eastern Roman Empire and address a serious question: Who is the Son, the second person of the Trinity? Recently, Ligonier Ministries offered snapshots of where Americans stand on certain theological ideas. To the statement, "Jesus was a great teacher, but he was not God," over 50 percent of those surveyed responded, "Strongly Agree" or "Somewhat Agree."[3] The souls of men and women depend on the correct answer to this and related questions.

Christians (more generally) and theologians (quite specifically) are tasked with contemplating divine mystery. We get to think about God, and this is a crucial activity of our spiritual life! We can only partially know and understand God, but even our limited acts of knowledge are deeply profound and invite the church into continual reflection on God and God's life—God's inner mysterious life and the eternal union of Father, Son, and Spirit. In the Christian life, we get to wonder, ponder, consider, contemplate, and sit still, apart from the ruminating chaos of our culture, and think about God.

As the church has contemplated God and God's life, theological formulations and a culture of theology have shaped our spiritual expression, theological framework, and missional impulse. As doctors of sacred things and doctors of the soul care for the church, the

---

[2] We unpack these observations in Coleman and Shawn J. Wilhite, *Ancient Wisdom for the Care of Souls: Learning the Art of Pastoral Ministry from the Church Fathers* (Crossway, 2024).

[3] Ligonier Ministries, 2022 Statement, The State of Theology, https://thestateoftheology.com/data-explorer/2022/7.

church receives medicine that tends to the deeper recesses of the person. Divine mystery and historical theological confessions about God coincide in the church's doctrine. We can reflect on one of the first ecumenical confessions of the church to mark her theological priorities: the Nicene Creed.

When medical doctors assess a patient, especially one without a clear diagnosis, they perform numerous tests, ask questions, and gather data. They approach solutions carefully, guided by the wisdom of a medical community. Doctors of the soul are no different. Those tasked with handling the mysteries of faith ought to take their work seriously and slowly. They must ask biblical questions, perform doctrinal tests, and gather soul data. They, too, must approach solutions carefully, guided by the spiritual wisdom of the historical Christian community. Christian theologians, like medical doctors, have a collective vocabulary conducive to good practice in describing a church community's doctrinal and spiritual maladies. Our Christian culture voices a desire for this specialized work, but, sadly, it does not always follow the correct prescriptions. John Webster observes, "Christian culture is the assembly of forms and practices which seeks somehow to inhabit the world which is brought into being by the staggering good news of Jesus Christ, the world of the new creation."[4] As doctors of sacred things, theologians and trained Christian leaders in the church bring Christians closer to this world of "staggering good news" and equip them to dwell in the divine life. To do this, we must remember the basic posture of the Christian life, in both doctrine and practice, is *always* one of faith and repentance.

Webster writes, "Faith is primary, because it's in faith that human life corresponds to the grace of God. Faith is that human

[4] John Webster, *The Culture of Theology* (Baker Academic, 2019), 43.

emptiness which lets God and God's work be, which receives what God is and what God does, [and] which says Yes to God's work of electing and judging and purifying."[5] Repentance is the response of a soul resting in faith. Repentance declares, "It's not heroics that matter; it's the much harder, much less-attractive business of letting God's judgment, God's claim, have priority in the way in which I order my life."[6] Theologians beckon the church back to her received faith and explain the faith in compelling ways to fit the time and occasion. In so doing, they also call the church to repent and wonder at the majesty of the triune God. So, theologians, including those who gathered at Nicaea, declare a truth about the soul we, too, often forget: "Trust and obey, for there is no other way to be happy in Jesus, but to trust and obey."[7]

The Necessity of Nicene Theology

The Council of Nicaea matters to our studies as historical theologians, but we also argue that the Creed of Nicaea matters to our faith today. The core Christian theology—the doctrine of God the Trinity, and the person and work of the eternal Son made flesh—is represented at the Council of Nicaea in 325. These Nicene doctrines and a few others—the person and work of the Spirit, the catholicity of the church, baptism, resurrection, and the eternal blessed life with God—were affirmed at Constantinople in 381. Since the medieval church, the language of these two events blended together so that the term "Nicene Creed" may now refer to the Creed of 325

---

[5] John Webster, *Confronted by Grace: Meditations of a Theologian* (Lexham, 2014), 172–73.

[6] Webster, 173.

[7] John H. Sammis, "Trust and Obey," Hymnary.org, https://hymnary.org/text/when_we_walk_with_the_lord (public domain).

and the Creed of 381.[8] We realize this muddies the waters, and we continue to wade in the mud. In this book, we refer to the Nicene Creed as both (1) the historical document originating in 325, and (2) the ecclesial document that assumes the creeds of both 325 and 381. Both the historical text and the collected ecclesial texts make up the tradition of Nicaea.

We have heard from others or have stories of our own of people who do not see the value or legitimacy of the Nicene Creed. One of our few goals in this book is to display the beauty of Nicene trinitarian theology as a vital and necessary theological creed for the modern Christian. We both come from free-church (or Low Church) backgrounds. We both remember when the Nicene Creed was foreign to our theological and spiritual formation. Now, the creed (alongside other ancient voices) shapes the theological vision of our personal lives, our homes, and the churches under our care. We hope evangelicals can appreciate and appropriate the fruit of Nicene Christianity for more vibrant Christian lives.

The Nicene Creed is a theological reflection by the church upon the Scriptures, structured as idiomatic phrases that foster memory and recitation, which depends on, coheres with, and, in turn, aids the reading of Scripture in the life of the church. The Nicene Creed (i.e., the Creed of 325) and the Niceno-Constantinople Creed (i.e., the Creed of 381) are theological reflections on the Trinity and other essential doctrines (soteriology, ecclesiology, and eschatology) that mark out the necessary theological beliefs of the Christian faith. The introductory phrases *credo* (I believe) and *credemus* (we believe) indicate that the creed is believed,

---

[8] For more on this history, see Wolfram Kinzig, *A History of Early Christian Creeds* (De Gruyter, 2024).

confessed by the church, and focused on specific, essential topics in its proclamations.

The Nicene Creed possesses authority insofar as it is a theological expression of the church's reading of the Scriptures. We want to press this discussion one step further to observe how the Spirit guides and moves the church in her faithfulness. The authority of Nicaea comes not from direct inspiration of God (as do the Scriptures), though we are sympathetic to this idea, but from the creed's origins: centuries-long affirmations, diverse ecclesial commitments, and true ecumenicism. As time progresses and the creed is defended and reaffirmed in each subsequent generation, the Nicene Creed grows in its authority because it has been (1) tested over and over again, (2) affirmed universally by all Christians, and (3) believed regardless of cultural boundaries.

This creedal authority fits within the framework of a Tradition 1 understanding, where we would also situate ourselves. Heiko A. Oberman defines the two-tradition model: Tradition 1 and Tradition 2.[9] We add, as others frequently have, a Tradition 0 distinction:

> Tradition 0: Scripture is the sole source for the church with no use of tradition.
>
> Tradition 1: Scripture is the sole source for the church with the aid and service of tradition.
>
> Tradition 2: Scripture and tradition possess equal authority for the life of the church.

---

[9] Heiko A. Oberman, *The Harvest of Medieval Theology: Gabriel Biel and Late Medieval Nominalism* (Baker Academic, 2000 [repr.; 1963]), 365–93. Also see Oberman, *Forerunners of the Reformation: The Shape of Late Medieval Thought*, Library of Ecclesiastical History (James Clarke Lutterworth, 2002).

The relationship between these three are complex, and each model includes an internal web of ideas. They ask, What is the rule for the life of the church? The Scriptures are the *norma normans* (the norming norm) and the creed is the *norma normata* (the normed norm). In other words, the Scriptures remain the ultimate source and guide for the church, while the creed is the theological expression of the guiding rule. Reflecting on the Reformation, scholar J. Todd Billings suggests that the Reformers "saw themselves in continuity with the early ecumenical councils and creeds of the church" and "saw it [the Nicene Creed] as a legitimate, catholic standard for them."[10] Billings further reflects on Nicene sensibilities in modern interpretations of the Scriptures: "We either use a Nicene preconception in interpreting Scripture (which you probably do if your church worships Jesus Christ as the Son, as well as the Spirit) or we don't. . . . All readers inhabit a Nicene or non-Nicene tradition of reading Scripture, whether they recognize it or not."[11]

The fourth-century Christian era displayed many principles essential to the classical trinitarian and Christological dogma, and contributed to the formation of several creedal confessions. Modern theologians and the church as a whole can still use these features as starting points for communicating these doctrines.[12] To this end, we aim to understand the historical and theological context of the council. We seek to know and to elucidate the Nicene theology as depicted within the creed itself. As any student of early Christianity

---

[10] J. Todd Billings, *The Word of God for the People of God: An Entryway to the Theological Interpretation of Scripture* (Eerdmans, 2010), 133. When we use the language of "catholic," we have in mind the Greek term, *katholikos*, which simply means "general" or "universal." All Christians are part of the church catholic.

[11] Billings, 49.

[12] Lewis Ayres, *Nicaea and Its Legacy: An Approach to Fourth-Century Trinitarian Theology* (Oxford University Press, 2004), 1.

knows, there were several debates about and interpretations of the creed. Therefore, we consciously align ourselves with the culture (*habitus*) of pro-Nicene theology: scriptural exegesis, theological explorations, a spiritual and virtuous life, and study of the controversies for sharper theological clarity.[13]

Of course, we are not living in the fourth century, but with each generation's challenges, the church's traditions are preserved and passed along to others, and must again be rediscovered. As Khaled Anatolios notes, "We cannot ignore the historical development and gain direct access to the object referents of the normative statements of trinitarian doctrine; we must creatively re-perform the acts of understanding and interpretation that led to those statements."[14] We self-identify as pro-Nicene theologians because of our (1) commitment to, preservation of, and desire to continue the Nicene formula; (2) trinitarian commitments; and (3) attempts to embody a scriptural reading *habitus*.

We affirm pro-Nicene theology as defined by Lewis Ayres in three unifying principles:

1. a clear version of the person and nature distinction, entailing the principle that whatever is predicated of the divine nature is predicated of the three persons equally and understood to be one (this distinction may or may not be articulated via a consistent technical terminology);

---

[13] In our book, *Ancient Wisdom for the Care of Souls*, we use the term *habitus* to refer to a culture and ingrained habits. As mentioned in the preceding paragraph, we desire others to *embody the culture* of pro-Nicene theologians who read Scripture in a particular way. See Coleman M. Ford and Shawn J. Wilhite, *Ancient Wisdom for the Care of Souls: Learning the Art of Pastoral Ministry from the Church Fathers* (Crossway, 2024).

[14] Khaled Anatolios, *Retrieving Nicaea: The Development and Meaning of Trinitarian Doctrine* (Baker Academic, 2011), 1.

2. clear expression that the eternal generation of the Son occurs within the unitary and incomprehensible divine being;
3. clear expression of the doctrine that the persons work inseparably.[15]

By aligning with these commitments, we offer insights tethered to the long thread of doctrinal reflection represented in the fourth-century pro-Nicene theological discourse. What happened at Nicaea was not meant to stay there but to reverberate in the halls of church history and across each horizon of Christian culture.

Where Are We Heading? An Overview of the Book

This book arises from years of reflection, conversation, writing, and reading about the Council of Nicaea, the aftermath of Nicaea, and the trajectories of pro-Nicene Christianity. Neither of us come from a High Church tradition, but we suppose that is exactly why we are continually drawn to Nicaea (and early Christianity in general). We have been influenced by Catholic, Orthodox, and Protestant scholars who continue to work in similar fields of study, including Khaled Anatolios, Lewis Ayres, Michel Barnes, and John Behr. Many people have dedicated their academic lives to understanding and unpacking the history, theology, and hermeneutics surrounding Nicaea. We simply join this chorus and rest on the shoulders of these giants, encouraging you to explore their work on this topic. We hope to bring to light their insights and apply them so that you understand the biblical foundations of Nicaea and why this creed still matters today. We hope to honor the work of these and other scholars who have advanced the topic of Nicene Christianity within

[15] Ayres, *Nicaea and Its Legacy*, 236.

the academy and the church. We hope to lean a little more on the former (i.e., academic scholarship) while remaining tethered to the work of the latter (i.e., ministry to the church). The modern church needs more anchors, not fewer, to the beauty and biblical fidelity represented at Nicaea.

In chapters 1 and 2, we unpack some of the historical and theological contexts that led to Nicaea. These chapters give you a snapshot into the world of the late third- and early fourth-century church, including key ecclesiastical and political figures. Chapters 3 and 4 explore the divinity and humanity of the Son, according to Nicaea. Here, we seek to outline a biblical understanding of the eternal generation of the Son and the relationship between Christ's humanity and his divinity. Chapters 5 and 6 explore the wonder of salvation and sanctification in Nicene terms. Looking at thinkers such as Athanasius of Alexandria, we explore the profundity of the gospel and its effects on our lives. Finally, in chapters 7 and 8, we offer several ways to use the creed in the life of the church and specify how it shapes our understanding of scriptural exegesis and theological discourse. We want you to see the Nicene Creed as a friend and a guide pointing the way to life on the map of Scripture.

In each chapter, you will see a relevant point titled "Thinking Nicenely Today." More than just the thesis of the chapter, this point is the big idea we ask you to ponder. In "Biblical Connection" sections, we consider key passages of Scripture and highlight modern commentators to connect our historical and theological discussion to the Word. Webster poignantly said, "Theology has its controlling center in exegesis of Holy Scripture; Holy Scripture is the Word of God; the Word of God summons us to faithful reading."[16] We hope we have presented such a faithful reading.

---

[16] Webster, *The Culture of Theology*, 65.

PART 1

The Context and Nicaea

CHAPTER 1

"There Was a Time When He Was Not": The Road to Nicaea

> But, as for those who say, "There was a time when he was not," and "before he was begotten, he was not," and that he came to be from nothing, or from a different hypostasis or substance, [who] claim that the Son of God is either [created or] mutable or alterable—The catholic and apostolic church anathematizes these people!
>
> —THE NICENE CREED (325)

> Guard the good deposit through the Holy Spirit who lives in us.
>
> —2 TIMOTHY 1:14

Thinking Nicenely Today: Though the truth of the Son's eternal life and complete divinity has been central to Christianity from its beginning, the trinitarian disputes of the third century and the controversy between Arius and Alexander awakened and sharpened the church's theological grammar. Eternal generation and the same divine substance stood at the heart of the Christological controversies at Nicaea in 325. The church must always point back to the fourth-century witness to address each subsequent trinitarian controversy that arises among us.

As a kid, I (Coleman) remember staying home from school on sick days, curled up on the couch, and watching *The Price Is Right* and reruns of *Family Ties* and *Different Strokes*. (If you are unfamiliar with any of these shows, stop reading now and look them up!) I also remember seeing a good deal of commercials for local law firms. One lawyer always stood out to me. He had given himself the nickname "The Texas Hammer." He would appear on-screen smashing things to illustrate how he would enact justice on your behalf. Even as an elementary school student, I chuckled at this and thought, *How silly*. As an adult, I rediscovered this commercial (yes, he is still around and smashing things), and realized The Texas Hammer is a marketing genius. He does not have to be a good lawyer; he only needs you to make the call. He hooks you with a no-nonsense persona and bold rhetoric, presenting himself as the only one who can fix your problems, make your life better, and get the justice ("million-dollar settlement") you deserve. If you believe he—and he alone—has the answers, the truth doesn't really matter. Rhetoric, with a bit of flash and machismo, matters most.

In the deserts of ancient Alexandria, a similar "hammer" made an impression on the hearts of his listeners. While he may have lacked the polish and brashness of a Texas lawyer, this man exhibited similar rhetorical skills and a bit of spiritual pizazz. He offered compelling answers to central questions of the Christian faith. And though he did not have a nickname, he composed captivating songs about his theology to further embed his ideas into the minds of listeners. His name was Arius.

Meeting Arius

When teaching church history and theology, I (Coleman) train my students to audibly gasp when they hear the name of Arius or see it written on the board. While I am being a bit humorous, I also help students understand that some names are so notorious in church history that they are worth gasping over. Historians face a conundrum when it comes to Arius of Alexandria: The main portrait we have of him was painted by his opponents. Rowan Williams observes, "By the early medieval period, we find him represented alongside Judas [Iscariot] in ecclesiastical art. . . . No other heretic has been through so thoroughgoing a process of 'demonization.'"[1] To be sure, Judas is not typically someone you want to be associated with in church history.

Historians must carefully extract what they can from the available sources, accounting for the fact that Arius's enemies were not always concerned with an accurate and fair representation. For instance, Athanasius of Alexandria and church historian Sozomen both depict Arius dying in a lavatory. This is certainly not a glamorous portrait, and their exact accounts are likely inaccurate.[2] There are far fewer sources about Arius's life and influences than one would hope. Only a few of his writings survive, constructed primarily out of second-hand quotations of others and leaving some doubt about their validity.[3] After surveying

[1] Rowan Williams, *Arius: Heresy and Tradition* (Eerdmans, 2001), 1.

[2] *De Morte Arii* 3.1–3.

[3] For a recent translation of Arius's letters to Eusebius of Nicomedia and Alexander of Alexandria, see Mark DelCogliano, trans., "Arius, Letters

numerous accounts, Williams concludes, "We are left with yet another of those tantalizing possibilities hovering on the margin of what we can securely know of Arius."[4] That said, most historians are confident in a general depiction of his life and theology in the available sources:

1. Arius was a presbyter in Alexandria under the jurisdiction of the bishop Alexander.
2. His teaching emphasized that Jesus was to be exalted as Lord but did not retain the same divine nature as God the Father.
3. He defined God the Father as a unitary being, wholly other, and denied the possibility that the Son was like the Father in all things regarding his divinity.
4. He was a spiritually pious individual, which lent credibility to his teaching.
5. His thought represents a wider and growing debate regarding the Son.

Early in the fourth century, Arius began teaching that the Son was not the eternally generated Son of the Father and, therefore, not the coequal and coeternal Son of God. To help spread this teaching, he even wrote songs that incorporated his belief about the Son: "There was a time when he was not."[5] These songs were, as Williams puts it, "dinner party songs" and easily

---

to Eusebius of Nicomedia and Alexander of Alexandria" in *The Cambridge Edition of Early Christian Writing*, vol. 1, *God*, ed. Andrew Radde-Gallwitz (Cambridge University Press, 2017), 110–13.

[4] Williams, *Arius*, 40.

[5] For a perspective on a theological and hymnic response to Arius from Ambrose of Milan (c. 339–397), see Coleman M. Ford, "The Pro-Nicene Hymns of Ambrose: A Pastoral Response to Arianism" *Southwestern Journal of Theology* 66.1 (Fall 2023): 47–68.

memorized.[6] Arius was charismatic, able to exert a high measure of pastoral authority outside the authority of his Bishop Alexander.[7] His ideas were the tip of an iceberg that drifted along in Christianity's waters for the next century, causing many spiritual shipwrecks. They are inherently dangerous theological ideas, especially because he could "prove" his conclusions from Scripture. This leads us to an important reality regarding biblical interpretation: *How* you read the text is more important than *how much* of the text you read. While the church does need more biblical literacy and intake of scripture, we desire to call attention to what we *do* with the Scriptures.

According to Arius, the Father is without a beginning, but the Son had a beginning at some point. Arius generally affirmed that the Son is still immutable and unchanging, yet unequal to the Father. Therefore, he reasoned, there must have been a time when God would not have been called "Father."[8] Consequently, the Son cannot see the Father perfectly or accurately. Additionally, Arius considered the Spirit as the first of the creatures made by the Son, who therefore does not share the nature of the Father or Son. Donald Macleod summarizes the issue with Arius's beliefs:

---

[6] Rowan Williams, "Athanasius and the Arian Crisis," *The First Christian Theologians: An Introduction to Theology in the Early Church,* ed. G. R. Evans (Blackwell, 2004), 161.

[7] Lewis Ayres, *Nicaea and its Legacy: An Approach to Fourth-Century Trinitarian Theology* (Oxford University Press, 2004), 16. Ayres notes that "even while Alexandria moved towards a monarchical model, it apparently maintained a tradition of independent priests whose relationship with the bishop was complex."

[8] Athanasius of Alexandria argues for this very idea in *de Decretis*. See Amy Brown Hughes and Shawn J. Wilhite, "The Beginnings of a Pro-Nicene Trinitarian Vision: Athanasius of Alexandria on the Activity of the Son and the Spirit," in *On Classical Trinitarianism: Retrieving the Nicene Doctrine of the Triune God*, ed. Matthew Barrett (IVP Academic, 2024).

> Qualifications of this kind naturally had the effect of confusing the faithful and prolonging the controversy. After all, it could be said, Arius' Christ was a magnificent being; and the role Arius ascribed to him in creation could even claim the support of Scripture. . . . The idea of the Son as a mediating creature is redolent only of Gnosticism, as if it were beneath the dignity of the true God to meddle with matter in the dirty business of creating.[9]

Arius wove his theological arguments from a web of biblical texts. First, he noted how Prov 8:22–31 spoke of the beginning of wisdom, personifying Wisdom as one of God's created agents, and that 1 Cor 1:24 calls the Christ the Wisdom of God.[10] He reasons that since wisdom is described in the Old Testament as created by God, and Christ is the Wisdom of God, then Christ must be a created agent of God. Surely, Arius's reading all makes biblical sense now, right? If you are feeling a bit queasy, you are not alone.

If the Son is a creature, albeit the highest creature, then this idea must show up elsewhere in Scripture, right? Here is where the analogy of the hammer comes in. Arius considered every passage that seems to depict Christ as lesser than the Father a nail to strike. Paul spoke of Christ as the "firstborn over all creation" in Col 1:15. *Whack!* In John 14:28, Jesus declares, "The Father is greater than I." *Bam!* Jesus stated in Mark 13:32 that even he did not know when the end would come. *Bang!* Anytime Jesus could be interpreted as

---

[9] Donald Macleod, *The Person of Christ*, ed. Gerald Bray, Contours of Christian Theology (IVP Academic, 1998), 122–23.

[10] For more on this see the discussion in Lewis Ayres, "Scripture in the Trinitarian Controversies," in *The Oxford Handbook of Early Christian Biblical Interpretation*, ed. Paul M. Blowers and Peter W. Martens (Oxford University Press, 2019), 439–54.

less than God and more like a creature, Arius's hammer strikes with a seemingly forceful theological blow.

The problem is not that Arius read the Bible but *how* he read it. Relatedly, Arius and his ideas prove that who you are—your character—influences how you read the Scriptures. Arius brings the wrong presuppositions to his Scripture reading, prohibiting him from correctly reading the Scriptures in light of the Son. We also bring a presupposition to the text—that the Son is eternally begotten and not made—but we argue that it is the *correct* presupposition. When you read Scripture while applying the notion that the Son is eternally begotten of the Father and of the same nature, you read the Scripture correctly and verify an orthodox presupposition. If you instead read like Arius, you presuppose different, non-Nicene theological commitments.[11] It certainly remains a topic for discussion: Should we assume theological ideas before we read a Bible passage? We answer with a resounding yes, though we acknowledge that Scripture and the Nicene heritage continue to shape these ideas.[12] We recognize a circular argument of the best sort: (1) Assume sound theology when reading Scripture. (2) Read Scripture to further develop sound theology. (3) Rinse and repeat. Thus, the Nicene Creed functions as guardrails to correct Scripture reading.

Arius and similar thinkers affirmed God's absolute divinity and self-existence. God the Father is uncaused and unoriginated

---

[11] This is why groups like the Jehovah's Witnesses have produced their own translation of the Bible, like the New World Translation, which translates texts such as John 1 in a way to make the Son appear less than fully God.

[12] For a helpful introduction to premodern exegesis and the need to assume theological categories alongside reading the Scriptures see Brandon D. Smith, *Taught by God: Ancient Hermeneutics for the Modern Church* (B&H Academic, 2024).

(Gr., *agenetos*), while the Son's divinity and lordship were conferred at a time after he came into being. They argued that some of Christ's titles—"Word," "Wisdom," and "Power of God"—indicate a lower level of divinity. Thus, the Son is not *agenetos* nor equal to the unoriginated Father. An early supporter of Arius, Eusebius of Nicomedia (d. ca. 342), "emphasized the divine title 'unbegotten' . . . as applicable only to one [the Father]" and was "wary of any language of communication of [divine] substance as suggesting . . . a materialistic fragmentation."[13] In Eusebius's view, the concept of the Son as the unbegotten one ruptures the very nature of God himself. Khaled Anatolios summarizes:

> If even in his divinity, this Word and Wisdom was caused—inasmuch as he was "begotten"—then he is in the last analysis a creature. Moreover, to say that he was altogether caused was to say that he came into existence from non-being, like all other creatures, through the sovereign will of the one uncaused God. In Arius' infamous slogan, "there was once when the Son was not." Nevertheless, he was unique as the first and highest creature, who was created to be the obedient instrument of all of God's subsequent creative activity. His unity with the God he called "Father" is therefore a unity of will and activity, not a unity of substance.[14]

In summary, according to Arius, the Son is not unoriginated and had a beginning; he is a dependent creature with an honorary title

---

[13] Khaled Anatolios, *Retrieving Nicaea: The Development and Meaning of Trinitarian Doctrine* (Baker Academic, 2011), 18.

[14] Khaled Anatolios, "Christology in the Fourth Century" in *The Oxford Handbook of Christology*, ed. Francesca Aran Murphy (Oxford University Press, 2015), 109.

of "Son." In his own words, Arius asserted, "by the will of God he was created before times and before ages and he has received his life, being, and glories from the Father, since the Father brought them into subsistence with him."[15]

Arius and Arianism(s)

We must take care when we speak of "Arianism" in the fourth century. Williams observes, "'Arianism' as a coherent system, founded by a single great figure and sustained by his disciples, is a fantasy."[16] In broad strokes, it is a term and a theology to be avoided, but many expressions emerged in the fourth century that require nuance and discernment. No theological label ("Calvinist," "Arminian," "Dispensational," etc.), has a one-size-fits-all definition. While a label like "Arianism" may be hard to avoid, it rarely does justice to the thoughts, influence, or theology of a specific individual or group.

In theological discourse, we need to be careful to avoid overextending terms. Arius did not espouse everything now called "Arianism." Additionally, no theological group in the fourth century consciously preserved Arius's writings or teachings. As with many so-called heresies, modern "orthodox" groups use the personal names of heretics to categorize contemporary ideas. Self-proclaimed followers of ancient thinkers build on similar foundations, taking their names to represent modern theological views. While Arius wove a consistent thread throughout his teaching, those who later took certain cues from his thought do not espouse the same theology in the same manner.

---

[15] Arius, *Letter to Alexander,* 3.

[16] Williams, *Arius*, 82.

Different shades of "Arianism" and ideas akin to Arius's developed after his time. The title "Arian" was certainly not desirable in the fourth century, and teachers with views friendly to Arian theology were quick to deny any association. Lewis Ayres traces the various Christological trajectories of the early fourth century, noting diverse thought and nuance in articulations of the relationship between the Father and Son.[17] Different descriptions of the Son's essence or substance distinguished certain ideas from the core of Arius's teaching before, during, and especially after the Council of Nicaea.[18] Thus, the term "Arianism" is not as helpful as once assumed. We ought to focus less on Arianism as a monolithic system and instead address any teaching that precludes the Son as eternally begotten and of the same essence as the Father.

Worshipping Jesus as God

Could Christ not do all the things we believe him to do even as a supreme being who is not fully God? In other words, could the Father not have just given the Son all the spiritual superpowers necessary to accomplish redemption? Why must the Christ really be fully God anyway? One crucial concept precludes this possibility: worship of God.

One powerful apologetic against Arian ideas is the liturgical legacy of the early church. It is clear from the New Testament and early church writings that Christians always worshipped Jesus as God. This is unthinkable if the Son made flesh is not fully God.

---

[17] Ayres, *Nicaea and its Legacy*, 41–84.

[18] For a helpful summary of different theological groups around the time of Nicaea, see J. Rebecca Lyman, "Arius and Arians" in *The Oxford Handbook of Early Christian Studies*, ed. Susan Ashbrook Harvey and David G. Hunter (Oxford University Press, 2008), 246–51.

Early Christians, many of whom were Jews, followed the command to give allegiance to God alone. They kept their monotheism and considered worship of anyone else idolatry. Larry Hurtado notes, "[The] conviction that Jesus had been exalted to heavenly status and power arose among pious Jews, people not easily disposed to accepting the idea of the deification of humans."[19] It is notable and even strange that these "pious Jews" worshipped the exalted Christ. Hurtado goes on to say, "Christ came to be included as an object of the devotional attention characteristically reserved for God in other examples of Jewish tradition. . . . they included Jesus in their religious devotion out of an apparent conviction that it was the will of the one God for them to do so and they saw their action as an affirmation of the sovereignty and glory of God."[20] This new allegiance to Christ does not automatically lead to the full Nicene declaration, "true God from true God," but, as Hurtado observes, the Jewish Christians departed sharply from their tradition by promptly devoting themselves to Jesus in the same way they had always devoted themselves to God.

Historical persecution of the church also evidences that Christians necessarily worship Christ as God. In the second century, Roman governor Pliny the Younger interrogated Christians. In one letter, Pliny recounts two deaconesses whom he detained and tortured to reveal the nature of their Christian gathering. He failed to coerce these women to renounce the name of Christ and instead worship the image of the emperor. These women told Pliny that their community gathered each Sunday to offer prayers, read their holy books, encourage one another toward

---

[19] Larry Hurtado, *One God, One Lord: Early Christian Devotion and Ancient Jewish Monotheism*, 3rd ed., The Cornerstones Series (T&T Clark, 2015), 103.

[20] Hurtado, 104.

good works, share a meal (likely the Lord's Supper), and sing hymns "to Christ as God."[21] Pliny was perplexed; it made no sense for these people to worship a crucified carpenter. What he considered a vain superstition, the early Christians worshipped as the very object of adoration.

Christians in the early centuries were ridiculed and condemned because of their worship of Christ. Many Christians are being so treated today. If Jesus were simply one of many divine beings, it would be much easier to adjust Christian practice according to the surrounding culture. Christ is not just *a* divine being; he is *the* divine being. All worship, glory, and honor are due to him, and anything less was unimaginable to the early Christians. It must remain so today. These early believers were committed to the worship of Christ to the point of death. If worship is due to God alone, then their commitment makes sense, but if one could worship every so-called divine being equally, then their suffering was for nothing. True devotion to the eternal Word made flesh as God is not optional to Christian faith; it is at the central core of Christian belief.

Arius's formulation assumes that Christ was worthy of honor but could not be fully worthy of worship. Phillip Cary picks up on this theme: "That would mean he is not really God at all, but one of the things God made. To say this would be to say that what Christians have been doing all along, worshiping Jesus as Lord, is the kind of thing pagans do: worshiping something that is not fully, truly, ultimately God."[22] If the Son is anything less than God, he is not owed full allegiance. Early Christians were not naive. They were not uninformed. They extolled God in Christ and devoted

---

[21] Pliny the Younger, *Letter* 10.96 in P. G. Walsh, trans., *Pliny the Younger: Complete Letters* (Oxford University Press, 2006), 278–79.

[22] Phillip Cary, *The Nicene Creed: An Introduction* (Lexham, 2023), 2.

themselves to the true worship of God made flesh for our salvation. A commitment to Christ as God is an undeniable fact of early Christian life and belief.

Biblical Connections

While the Council of Nicaea and its surrounding events are situated in history, they are not disconnected from biblical reflection. The early church did not rely on proof texts but read and interpreted the whole Bible. Though there are clear texts about Jesus and his divinity, no passage ought to be read in isolation. With that in mind, here are some key biblical texts for reflection upon Arius and the initial context that sparked Nicaea.

When considering the person and teaching of Arius, recall the numerous statements in the pastoral epistles warning the church to weigh the character and theology of false teachers. Paul wrote to Timothy that right doctrine and good character go together. He warned that some teachers go astray into "fruitless discussion" (1 Tim 1:6). Others see ministry as an avenue for "material gain" (1 Tim 6:5). Teachers who do not "agree with the sound teaching of our Lord Jesus Christ and with teaching that promotes godliness" are "conceited and [understand] nothing" (1 Tim 6:3–4). Indeed, their minds are "depraved and deprived of the truth" (1 Tim 6:5). Paul noted that the hallmark of a false teacher is strife and dissension in the church.

Near the end of his life, Paul commanded, "Hold on to the pattern of sound teaching that you have heard from me, in the faith and love that are in Christ Jesus. Guard the good deposit through the Holy Spirit who lives in us" (2 Tim 1:13–14). Paul emphatically charged Timothy to teach good doctrine. "Sound teaching" translates literally to "healthy words"; these are more than just pleasant words, "but a saving and life-transforming body of doctrine."[23] Every teacher in the church must, like Timothy, pass down the apostolic doctrine of Christ to the next generation. Anyone trusted with God's Word for God's people must take the ministry of guardianship seriously. Shepherds can only do this in the power of the Spirit. In both of his letters to Timothy, Paul warns of general threats to sound doctrine and specific people who spiritually ransack the church with false teachings. Timothy, Paul instructed, must be on guard and lean on the Holy Spirit in his ministry of teaching and caring for the saints. John Stott agrees, "There were heretics abroad, bent on corrupting the gospel and so robbing the church of the priceless treasure which had been entrusted to it. Timothy must be on the watch."[24]

The saints of God are strengthened by the consistent and faithful teaching of biblical doctrine. A church body also depends on its faithful shepherd, the pastor, who leads with a humble heart and nurtures their souls by his contemplation of God in Christ through prayer and biblical meditation. He leads by both following Christ and guarding Christ's teachings, and by watching over both his own life and the teachings of the church. The shepherd cares about virtue and spirituality, theology and instruction. He works to ensure he personally follows the sound teaching of Scripture and teaches in accordance with the hope of the gospel. Your leaders should not be teaching you any brand-new theology. A faithful shepherd gives new connections and new ways to understand a biblical truth, but his message ought to remain: Follow the sure pattern of Christ and trust in the deposit of faith given to you in him.

---

[23] Robert W. Yarbrough, *The Letters to Timothy and Titus*, The Pillar New Testament Commentary (Eerdmans, 2018), 365.

[24] John R. W. Stott, *Guard the Gospel: The Message of 2 Timothy*, The Bible Speaks Today (IVP, 1973), 44.

Conclusion

A popular meme circulates once a year or so that we call "Saint Nicholas: The Heretic Puncher." We both have a particular affinity for this meme and occasionally text it to one another. There are various (and admittedly hilarious) versions of this meme. Each version includes an image of the historical Saint Nicholas (as he is depicted by Eastern Orthodox iconography) punching or slapping Arius at the Council of Nicaea. We particularly like iterations that reference Saint Nicholas as the inspiration for Santa Claus, such as the one shown on the Libertarian Catholic website. Emblazoned across the top and bottom of the meme are the words "St. Nicholas: I only came to give presents to kids and punch heretics and I just ran out of presents."[25] While it is amusing at Christmas to imagine "Santa" in this way, this event likely did not happen.[26] Still, the meme abides and teaches us the positive lesson that orthodox Christians ought to care deeply about the spiritual consequences of lousy teaching and shoddy biblical interpretation. Arius represents a growing question in the early church: How do we faithfully understand the person and work of the eternal Son of God made flesh?

As a concluding word, while we disagree with Arius and the numerous theological iterations that followed his line of thought, we must be careful in our use of the words "heretic" and "heresy" in public discourse. We recognize that one person's heresy may be another person's orthodoxy. As Protestant evangelicals and as Baptists, we understand some may consider *us* heretics. As Christ-followers, we

---

[25] See The Libertarian Catholic, December 5, 2018, https://thelibertariancatholic.com/st-nicholas-i-only-came-to-give-presents-to-kids-and-punch-heretics-and-i-just-ran-out-of-presents/.

[26] For a brief but helpful assessment of the myth of Saint Nick punching Arius at Nicaea, see Michael Svigel and John Adair, *Urban Legends of Church History: 40 Common Misconceptions* (B&H Academic, 2020), 52.

must make it our priority to affirm the essentials of Christian faith with other brothers and sisters in Christ while charitably discussing our differences on important, yet less essential, doctrinal matters.[27] We affirm what Jesus declared to his disciples in Mark 9:40–41, "For whoever is not against us is for us. And whoever gives you a cup of water to drink in my name, because you belong to Christ—truly I tell you, he will never lose his reward."

Even with doctrinal differences, all Christians must aim to represent the full biblical portrait of Jesus Christ, guard the deposit of life-giving words about Christ, and winsomely address the accretions of error that can develop over time. Wrong teaching and weak exegesis lead to bad ideas, and potentially ruin spiritual lives. God plainly commanded us to "hold fast" to the truth (1 Thess 5:21; Heb 4:14; 10:23). As we consider the early landscape of Nicaea, our primary and ongoing concern must be adherence to biblical truth.

[27] Two helpful works on this topic are Gavin Ortlund, *Finding the Right Hills to Die On: The Case for Theological Triage* (Crossway, 2020), and Rhyne R. Putman, *When Doctrine Divides the People of God: An Evangelical Approach to Doctrinal Diversity* (Crossway, 2020).

CHAPTER 2

"By This Sign, Conquer": Constantine and the Council of Nicaea

> We believe in one God, the Father Almighty,
> Maker of all things both visible and invisible.
>
> —The Nicene Creed (325)

> Honor everyone. Love the brothers and sisters. Fear God. Honor the emperor.
>
> —1 Peter 2:17

Thinking Nicenely Today: Christians must never rely on earthly rulers to solve spiritual and theological issues. However, God uses the most unlikely people and events to prompt the church to reflect on her theological and ethical commitments.

The Nicene Creed begins with a declaration of faith in God the Father Almighty; it does not beckon us to give allegiance to an earthly ruler, kingdom, or government. Though we are to honor governing authorities, God alone is owed our first and lasting fidelity. Christian leaders must not deny their allegiance to Christ. Several Christians in the early centuries of the church were alarmingly comfortable with earthly rulers addressing the ecclesiastical and theological affairs of the church.

The early fourth century was a time of great upheaval. The system of four imperial rulers devised by the emperor Diocletian in the late third century to bring stability, known as the Roman tetrarchy, was crumbling under the weight of authoritarian greed. The once seemingly eternal Roman Empire looked less and less immortal with each passing decade.[1] In certain religious groups, particularly the Christian church, empire-wide persecution claimed many lives and harmed countless more.[2] The world needed a larger-than-life figure to put things back together and restore Rome; that person was Constantine the Great.

Whether he was as great as his epithet suggests, Emperor Constantine I made sweeping changes to the Roman Empire. We will discuss the pros and cons of Constantine's legacy, but to put it simply, no Constantine, no Nicaea.[3] Before we attempt to understand Constantine, we need to understand the background and

---

[1] For a helpful summary of this period leading up to Constantine, see Simon Corcoran, "Before Constantine" in *The Cambridge Companion to the Age of Constantine*, ed. Noel Lenski (Cambridge University Press, 2006), 35–58.

[2] Wolfram Kinzig, *Christian Persecution in Antiquity*, trans. Markus Bockmuehl (Baylor University Press, 2021).

[3] See Raymond Van Dam, "Imperial Fathers and their Sons" in *Cambridge Companion to the Council of Nicaea*, ed. Young Richard Kim (Cambridge University Press, 2021), 19–42.

context that preceded him. We must begin with what many historians call the Crisis of the Third Century.[4]

Crisis and Christian Persecution

The third century was a bit of a mess in the Roman Empire. Natural disasters, plagues, civil war, foreign invasions, and a string of bad emperors (twenty-seven over the course of fifty years) culminated in what has since been called the Crisis of the Third Century. The term "crisis" may even be a bit of an understatement. In AD 284, the emperor Diocletian came to power and finally brought some stability to this mess of a century. Among many practical solutions, Diocletian instituted system-wide persecution of anyone who would not bow the knee to the image of the emperor. While emperor worship was not a full-fledged religious system, every good Roman contributed a small sacrifice of incense and prayer to the "genius," or interior spirit, of the emperor for the good of the empire.

Christians, however, could not obey the statute and bow to the emperor's image in good conscience. Stephen Presley observes that Christians had an "active political dualism," in which they recognized their heavenly citizenship but still prayed for leaders, paid taxes, and sought to encourage virtuous living for the public

---

[4] For a helpful treatment on this era of Roman political crisis in the third century, see Clifford Ando, *Imperial Rome AD 193 to 284: The Critical Century* (Edinburgh University Press, 2012). While avoiding the phrase "crisis of the third century," David Potter has a helpful summary of the numerous transitions taking place during the third and early fourth centuries leading to Constantine. See David S. Potter, "The Transformation of the Empire: 235–337 CE" in *A Companion to the Roman Empire*, ed. David S. Potter (Blackwell, 2006), 153–73.

good.[5] In the second century, the anonymous writer of a letter to a non-Christian named Diognetus described the life and virtue of Christians as follows: "They live in their own countries, but only as aliens; they participate in everything as citizens, and endure everything as foreigners. Every foreign country is their fatherland, and every fatherland is foreign. They marry like everyone else, and have children, but they do not expose their offspring. They share their food but not their wives."[6] Christian apologists throughout the early centuries argued that Christians were a force for good in Roman society, even if they could not participate in all the trappings of Roman culture. Christians were not anti-imperial, but neither did they embrace the full scheme of Roman political life with its profuse pagan practices. Their moral line was crossed when the empire demanded they worship anyone but Christ as Lord.

Diocletian's plan was both a civic and a moral revolution, and for it to succeed, he had to reemphasize Rome's traditional values. The Great Persecution of Diocletian began in AD 303 with a series of four imperial edicts over the course of a year:

> Edict one, given in February, encouraged the destruction of churches, burnings of Christian literature, and prohibition of Christian gatherings.
>
> Edict two (after February AD 303) imprisoned members of the clergy.
>
> Edict three (after February AD 303) released clergy members who had sacrificed to Roman deities.

---

[5] Stephen O. Presley, *Cultural Sanctification: Engaging the World like the Early Church* (Eerdmans, 2024).

[6] *Diogn.* 5.5–7. See translation in Michael W. Holmes, *The Apostolic Fathers: Greek Texts and English Translations*, Updated ed. (Baker Books, 1999), 541.

> Edict four (the beginning of AD 304) established a general obligation to make sacrifices to Roman deities.[7]

Anyone unwilling to conform to obligatory worship of the Roman gods was immediately persecuted and blamed for the deterioration of Roman society. Rejection of the Roman gods by groups such as the Christians must be the reason for Roman downfall, or so the argument went. The Christians and their claim of religious exclusivity supposedly disrupted the *pax deorum*, or "peace of the gods." The issue was made worse by Diocletian himself and his desire to style himself as a living god. Mandated worship of the emperor and the Roman gods eventually led to exclusive and systematic persecution of the church. Churches and copies of Scripture were burned. Clergy were targeted for torture, exile, and death.

During the Diocletian persecution, Eusebius recalled that "each underwent a series of varied forms of torture: one would have his body maltreated by scourgings; another would be punished with the rack and torn to an unbearable degree, whereat some met a miserable end to their life."[8] The Romans created new forms of punishment in their persecution of the Christians.[9] For example, a certain man was arrested because he refused to offer sacrifices. He was raised up naked, and his whole body was torn with scourges, with the hope that he would give in. The Romans then mixed vinegar and salt together and poured the mixture onto his body. Then, they made a gridiron (iron table) and slowly put the remnants of his dead body on it.[10] In one account, Eusebius mentions several other gruesome acts of Christian persecution:

---

[7] Kinzig, *Christian Persecution in Antiquity*, 161.

[8] Eusebius, *Eccl. Hist.* 8.3.1–2.

[9] Eusebius, *Eccl. Hist.* 8.6.1.

[10] Eusebius, *Eccl. Hist.* 8.6.2–4.

> They had the entire body torn to pieces with sharp shards instead of claws . . . Women were fastened by one foot and swung aloft through the air, head-downwards, to a height by certain machines, their bodies completely naked. . . . Others, again, were fastened to trees and trunks . . . For, they drew together by certain machines the very strongest of the branches, to each of which they fastened one of the martyr's legs, and then released the branches to take up their natural position.[11]

Eusebius noted that this practice was not done only for a few days but for years, and to up to 100 persons a day, ranging from young children, to women, to older men.[12]

Eusebius recounted a similar macabre moment of torture of a Christian man named Peter in Nicomedia. Sparing the gruesome details, Eusebius ended his account by saying, "But he stuck immovably to his determination, and victorious in the midst of his tortures, breathed his last. Such was the martyrdom of one of the imperial servants, a martyrdom worthy of the name he bore—it was Peter."[13] Similar stories could be recounted from across the empire through much of the late third and early fourth century. Such persecutions, however, were unsuccessful in eradicating the Christian faith. If anything, they only increased sympathy for Christians and conversions to the faith. By the time of Constantine as bishop of Rome, the Roman Empire had all but officially recognized that Christianity was here to stay. W. H. C. Frend notes, "The successive edicts of toleration issued by Maxentius

---

[11] Eusebius, *Eccl. Hist.* 8.9.1–2.

[12] Eusebius, *Eccl. Hist.* 8.9.3.

[13] Eusebius, *Eccl. Hist.* 8.6.4.

in Rome, by Galerius, Constantine and Licinius, and finally even by Maximian, set the seal on a process which had already run its course."[14]

Another part of Diocletian's reform included the introduction of the imperial tetrarchy, otherwise known as the rule of four. This system alleviated the confusion regarding imperial succession. Four rulers—a junior and a senior leader for the western half of the empire and a junior and senior for the eastern half—managed the administrative structure and provided stability. The junior emperor, Caesar, ruled alongside the senior leader, Augustus. When an Augustus retired, the junior was promoted to Augustus, and a new Caesar took his place. This system appeared to be working, at least for the first series of four rulers. Then, a man named Maxentius, the son of one of the original tetrarchs, assumed he was next in line but was left out. Additionally, Constantius, Constantine's father and Augustus in the west, died soon after his promotion and Constantine was proclaimed Augustus in his place. This not only bypassed the system, but it reintroduced the issue Diocletian was seeking to avoid—namely, the sudden establishment of an emperor by loyal troops.

Table 2.1. Imperial Tetrarchy (AD 293–305)

West	East
Maximian, Augustus	Diocletian, Augustus
Constantius, Caesar	Galerius, Caesar

[14] W. H. C. Frend, "The Failure of the Persecutions in the Roman Empire" *Past & Present*, 16 (November 1959): 27.

Fig. 2.1. *Portrait of the Four Tetrarchs*, a fourth-century porphyry statue, St. Mark's Cathedral, Venice, Italy (Wikipedia Commons; https://commons.wikimedia.org/wiki/File:Venice_%E2%80%93_The_Tetrarchs_03.jpg)

The Rise and Rule of Constantine

Constantine (c. 280–337) was born to Flavius Valerius Constantius and his wife (likely a concubine), Helena. Constantius was a high-ranking military officer who eventually rose to the rank of Caesar in the west under the system of imperial tetrarchy. Constantius, as any Roman with means and a desire for honor was apt to do, divorced his wife and married the stepdaughter of Maximian, the western Augustus. This marriage secured his son Constantine a place at the imperial court under the eastern Augustus, Diocletian. We know Constantine witnessed the debates and policy decisions related to the persecution of Christians by Diocletian in 303. After ascending to the rank of western Caesar, Constantius embarked on a series of military campaigns in Britain. Constantine accompanied his father, who died in 306 at a battle in York, and the army soon declared Constantine emperor. Caesar Galerius in the east accepted this decision and immediately shocked the system of tetrarchic rule, leading to civil strife. Maxentius, the son of the western Augustus Maximian, did not take kindly to being overlooked for imperial succession. When he heard how Constantine had gamed the system, he revolted, amassing an army in Rome and aligning with the eastern emperor Maximinus. Diocletian's solution to the imperial issue soon unraveled, leading Rome again into civil war.

Constantine and his eventual co-emperor Licinius thus found themselves at odds with other would-be imperial leaders. The two became allied for the purposes of consolidating power, yet Constantine would quickly become the more powerful of the two. In the images of Licinius (Fig. 2.2) and Constantine (Fig. 2.3), viewers can gauge the differences in the perceived stature of each leader. Constantine allied himself with Licinius to defeat what he perceived as the greater threat. As the old Latin saying goes, *Amicus meus, inimicus inimici mei*, or, "The enemy of my enemy is my friend." The two men would eventually author the so-called Edict of Milan, discussed momentarily. A few short years later, Licinius would find himself as the main threat standing in the way of Constantine's aspirations for sole imperial rule. Constantine would

Fig. 2.2. Bust of the emperor Licinius, Kunsthistorisches Museum. Wikimedia Commons. https://commons.wikimedia.org/wiki/File:Bust_of_Licinius,_Kunsthistorisches_Museum.jpg

Fig. 2.3. Colossus bust of Constantine, Casey Lovegrove, Unsplash. https://unsplash.com/photos/a-close-up-of-a-statue-of-a-mans-head-egJJQ4hUmp0

have his former ally executed following a crippling defeat at the Battle of Chrysopolis in 324.

AD 312–13 and the (Official?) End of Christian Persecution

Maxentius's designs for power came to an end at the famous Battle of Milvian Bridge in 312. This battle is depicted today on Constantine's Arch in Rome (see Fig. 2.4). Constantine was a capable military general and appears to have had the advantage on the battlefield: Maxentius left too little room between Constantine's troops and the River Tiber. This position made it hard for Maxentius's men to regroup for additional attacks. When Constantine seemed to have an advantage, Maxentius and his troops retreated via the Milvian Bridge over the Tiber, incurring many losses along the way. Maxentius perished with many of his troops in the river. Soon after his victory, Constantine marched into Rome and established himself as the sole ruler of the western Roman Empire. While it depends on the vantage point, this battle could be seen as divinely appointed or a strategic military event.

Fig. 2.4. The Arch of Constantine depicting the Defeat of Maxentius. Wikimedia Commons. (https://en.wikipedia.org/wiki/File:Luk_Konstantyna_6DSCF0032.JPG#filelinks)

Our primary Christian sources for this period come from Eusebius of Caesarea (c. 260/5–339) and Lactantius (c. 250–325).

Both men were present during Diocletian's persecution of Christians, and both witnessed Constantine's rise to the imperial throne. A revered rhetor and scholar, Lactantius was called by Diocletian to serve the imperial court as a rhetor in Nicomedia. Having converted to Christianity around this time, he left his post before Diocletian made his official edicts against Christians. Lactantius lived in obscurity for several years before Constantine later became his patron. Within the years 303–11, Lactantius wrote *The Divine Institutes*, his major work and an apology for the Christian faith and critique of pagan religion. The new emperor Constantine appointed Lactantius as tutor for his son, Crispus, in Gaul. Historians believe Lactantius served as an advisor of some sort to Constantine, perhaps influencing his imperial legislation, until Lactantius's death sometime around 325.[15]

Eusebius was a bishop in Caesarea and became an adviser and friend to Constantine. While Lactantius did not always live near Constantine, Eusebius consistently rubbed shoulders with the emperor until Constantine's death. The bishop even served as Constantine's ecclesiastical escort at the Council of Nicaea. Both Eusebius and Lactantius interpreted Constantine's success and rise to power using biblical terms. Eusebius in particular saw the beginning of a new Christian era for Rome in Constantine. His continual proximity to Constantine is evident in his writings, including in his panegyric dedicated to Constantine on the thirtieth anniversary of the emperor's accession in 336. In it, Eusebius unapologetically assigned divine favor to Constantine. He called the emperor,

---

[15] Vincenzo Loi and Biagio Amata, "Lactantius," ed. Angelo Di Berardino and James Hoover, trans. Joseph T. Papa, Erik A. Koenke, and Eric E. Hewett, *Encyclopedia of Ancient Christianity* (IVP Academic, 2014), 2:511.

"a lesson in the pattern of godliness to the human race" and a "huge luminary and loud-voiced herald of unerring godliness."[16]

Before issuing the Edict of Milan, according to Constantine's apologists, the emperor attributed his successes to the Christian God. Recounting the famous battle against Maxentius at the Milvian Bridge, Lactantius, in his *De mortibus persecutorum* (*On the Death of the Persecutors*) recalled: "Constantine was warned in quiet to mark the celestial sign of God on his shields and thus engage in battle. He did as he was ordered. He inscribed the name of Christ on the shields, using the initial letter X crossed with an I with its top portion bent. Armed with this sign, the army took the sword."[17] This symbol, the Chi-Rho (☧), combines the first two Greek letters in the word "Christ." Both Eusebius and Lactantius credit the Chi-Rho as the reason for Constantine's success and a visible turning point in both his life and his eventual rule of the Roman empire.

Some scholars see this Christian symbol of Constantine's success as evidence that he had conversed with Christian leaders before this time.[18] It was normal for leaders to invoke deities before battle, yet this event (if told accurately by later commentators) marks a decidedly new attitude in Rome toward Christianity. Whether or not Constantine received a vision directly from the Lord, we know that following this battle, the Christian church was no longer subject to official persecution in Rome and instead accrued favor from the very top members of Roman society. The Edict of Milan of

---

[16] *Life of Constantine* 4 in Averil Cameron and Stuart G. Hall, trans., *Eusebius: Life of Constantine*, Clarendon Ancient History Series (Clarendon Press, 1999), 69.

[17] Lactantius, *The Death of the Persecutors,* §44 in Mary Francis McDonald, trans. *Lactantius: The Minor Works,* The Fathers of the Church 54 (Catholic University of America Press, 1965), 190–91.

[18] Timothy Barnes, *Constantine: Dynasty, Religion and Power in the Later Roman Empire* (Wiley Blackwell, 2011), 80.

312/3, issued jointly by Licinius and Constantine soon after the Battle at the Milvian Bridge, officially ended Roman persecution of Christians and granted recognized status to the Christian faith.[19] An edict issued by the emperor Galerius two years prior had officially ended Christian persecution in the eastern empire. This initial edict was simply a statement of toleration, and Christians were not exactly favored nor lauded. The Edict of Milan fully restored property and rights to Christians and provided for state restitution, including tax-exempt status for Christian leaders. From this point on, Christianity was never the same.

Constantine began to give Christian leaders and nobility new and significant opportunities. The next thirty years witnessed a dramatic increase in ecclesial activity, both in church building construction and ecumenical gatherings (such as the Council of Nicaea).[20] The new so-called Christian emperor issued laws that favored clergy members, providing them with various fiscal and legal privileges. These changes radically transformed the position and authority of both the individual Christian church leaders and the very organization of the episcopacy.[21] Constantine increasingly viewed himself as a patron of the church as much as a patron of the empire; perhaps he even saw these two as synonymous. This new attitude in favor of Christianity and its potential to unify the

---

[19] Historians debate as to whether there was an official edict issued or whether it was simply an agreement made by the co-emperors.

[20] H. A. Drake, "The Impact of Constantine on Christianity" in *The Cambridge Companion to the Age of Constantine*, ed. Noel Lenski (Cambridge University Press, 2006), 111.

[21] Raymond van Dam, "Bishops and Society" in *The Cambridge History of Christianity: Volume 2, Constantine to c. 600*, ed. Augustine Casiday and Frederick W. Norris (Cambridge University Press, 2007), 343–44.

Roman Empire under Constantine's sole rule is most evident in his calling for a worldwide church council at Nicaea.

Constantine as a Christian Emperor (or Not?)

By Constantine's death in 337, most of the Roman Empire had been Christianized. This was a paradigm shift in world history, not to mention in church history. Could the Christian faith, once despised as a pariah to the Roman Empire, become the spiritual glue that binds the world together? Constantine believed so. His reign led to an influx of new people joining the church, which went from being a persecuted minority to an influential community favored by the highest authorities. Figures such as Eusebius of Caesarea credited this shift to the providence of God, insisting that the church and the state could function in harmony and that Constantine operated as a divine archetype who looked to heaven to pattern his government. This new era, which came to be known as "Constantinianism," ushered in a new reality for both the church and the state that remained the consistent pattern in the subsequent Byzantine Empire and various kingdoms of the medieval West.[22] This "Constantinian" view of church and state remained influential for centuries. But what can we say about Constantine's Christian faith? We offer a few cautionary observations.

---

[22] "Constantinianism" refers to a political ideology that envisions a closer union between Church and state. Such was the prevailing notion for much of European history following Constantine. Advocates for religious liberty, or the separation of the church and the state, regularly challenge the notion of Constantinianism. For a helpful overview of political theology, with compelling arguments for separation of church and state, from a free-church perspective, see Thomas S. Kidd, Paul D. Miller, and Andrew T. Walker, eds. *Baptist Political Theology* (B&H Academic, 2023).

First, a leader who favors the Christian church is not *de facto* a sincere believer in Christ. Evidence indicates that Constantine continued to adhere to traditional (pagan) Roman titles and did not dismantle pagan rites and religion in the empire. He treated Christ like another statue in the Roman Pantheon, even if the preferred one. Second, anyone who professes faith in Christ (including the leader of an empire) ought to embrace a biblical transformation of their conduct and morals. From the evidence we have, Constantine was just as prone to the basic wiles of imperial leadership as his predecessors, though perhaps to a lesser degree given his favor toward Christianity. He executed his enemies and people who threatened to claim the imperial throne. Finally, as evidenced in Constantine's age and ours, political leaders can provide favorable environments for Christian faith and practice out of self-seeking motivations. We should not be cynical or uncharitable, but neither should we be naive and misled. We can praise God when governments or rulers align with Christian priorities, but we must not trust them to always do so. Our trust must be in God, regardless of a politician's platform, rhetoric, or policy decisions. Constantine's motivations to hold the Council of Nicaea was as political as they were ecclesiological and theological.

Constantine championed the Council of Nicaea (325) to deal with the Arian heresy. It seems Constantine expected everyone to ascend to the new Creed, including Arius himself.[23] Constantine's disapproval of Arius appears to have abated following the Council of Nicaea, and the emperor's sister even helped restore Arius to imperial favor shortly before his death.[24] Additionally, Constantine

---

[23] Timothy D. Barnes, *Constantine and Eusebius* (Harvard University Press, 1981), 216.

[24] David Potter, *Constantine the Emperor* (Oxford University Press, 2013), 283.

was responsible for the exile of Athanasius of Alexandria in 336, who had been accused by Arian sympathizers of threatening to interfere with grain supplied from Egypt. The mediating nature of Constantine's ecclesiastical policy also appears in his deathbed baptism in 337, which was performed by Eusebius of Nicomedia, a man loosely sympathetic to Arian-like ideas.

The Timeline to Nicaea

Having surveyed Constantine's rise to power, including some markers of his life as emperor and a Christian, how should we understand his influence within the church and the Council of Nicaea? While the full timeline of events leading to Nicaea would require more space than we have here, the following are some notable developments:

1. Alexander, bishop of Alexandria, learns of Arius's problematic teaching (318/9)
2. Alexander issues the *heno sōmatos* (Gk. "one body") document as a theological declaration meant to address the teaching of Arius and others (319)
3. Arius submits a statement of his belief and teaching (320)
4. Various local synods debate the issue (320–22)
5. Arius and his supporters appeal to Constantine, and Constantine responds (324)
6. Constantine calls for the ecumenical council to meet, originally in Ancyra, and then in Nicaea (325)[25]

Constantine knew early on of the brewing theological controversy and employed numerous ecclesiastical leaders to advise him. By

---

[25] See also Rowan Williams, *Arius: Heresy and Tradition* (Eerdmans, 2001), 29–92.

providing funds for their travel and lodging, Constantine sponsored the first ecumenical council made of bishops from all over the known world. Importantly, the Council of Nicaea was not the first ever church council. Christian leaders gathered to decide important matters of faith and practice as early as the Jerusalem Council recorded in Acts 15, just fifteen to twenty years into the Christian movement. Many subsequent regional councils took place in the early centuries of the church dealing with theological and ecclesiastical matters. While these councils addressed larger theological questions, they often settled local issues particular to their region of churches. The Council of Nicaea included a new dimension: an ecumenical scope. J. N. D. Kelly writes, "The early fourth century is acclaimed as having inaugurated the transition to this new type of formulary, but like most other historical transitions it was not in fact quite so abrupt as it has seemed."[26] The proceedings of this council presided over by Emperor Constantine had worldwide implications that reverberated throughout history and reecho today.

Biblical Connections

To make a biblical connection to Constantine and the calling of the first worldwide council, we draw your attention to the ways Scripture calls the church to honor earthly rulers and pray for those in authority. In Romans 13, Paul commands the church to respect and honor the governing authorities placed over us. Yet this command does not entail uncritical acceptance. F. F. Bruce maintained: "It is plain from the immediate context, as from the general context of the apostolic writings, that the state can rightly command obedience only within the limits of the purposes for which it has

[26] J. N. D. Kelly, *Early Christian Creeds,* 3rd ed. (Routledge, 1972), 205.

been divinely instituted—in particular, the state not only may but must be resisted when it demands the allegiance due to God alone."[27] Certainly, the instance of a Christian emperor shocked many Romans. Whether a ruler professes Christ as Lord or not, the church is called to accept that ruler's authority as ordained by God, pray for leaders, and be a presence for good within their community. We must also abide by the basic requirements of citizenship and participation in government, so long as it does not transgress the Christian conscience. While we will likely never see any government leader call a church council in our own day, we must pray that God will grant wisdom to those in authority and that they do what is right in the eyes of the Lord.

We owe our primary allegiance to Christ. Nations rise and fall, but the Word of the Lord, the eternal Son, will stand forever. Insofar as a ruler does something to aid Christians, the church ought to give thanks. But we must never expect this to be the case in every instance. When the apostle Peter wrote, "Honor the emperor" (1 Pet 2:17), the situation for Christians was less than favorable. Christians in the first century were a minority group—albeit growing in number—and sometimes received attention but went on mostly ignored. Peter understood that Christian commitments include loving your neighbor and praying for your enemy (Matt 5:44–46; 22:39). But how should Christians honor a king or emperor, especially one hostile to the Christian way of life? We should honor leaders in light of the commands to honor everyone, love brothers and sisters, and fear God (1 Pet 2:17). Thomas Schreiner offers the following exhortation: "Believers should continue to respect and honor the emperor, even though they are free

[27] F. F. Bruce, *Romans: An Introduction and Commentary*, Tyndale New Testament Commentaries 6 (IVP, 1985), 236.

citizens of God. Their freedom should not become a pretext for sin, as if they were free from giving the emperor the respect the office deserved."[28] We ought to be cautious when accepting political favor of Christianity; yet, regardless of favor or lack of it, Christians must always give godly deference to our political leaders.

Conclusion

It is difficult for us to imagine how the church in Constantine's Rome so easily turned to an earthly emperor to help them solve a theological issue. No one saw Constantine as a theological leader, but some Christians looked to him as a divinely appointed arbiter in ecclesiastical disputes. We ought to be encouraged by those in positions of earthly authority who wish to lead with Christian conviction. The church should pray for every governing authority, whether local or national, regardless of their political affiliation. At the same time, we must be wary when such leaders wish to exert their authority in ecclesiastical affairs. We can simultaneously recognize how Constantine played a pivotal role in solving a major theological debate and advocate for restraint in mixing politics with the church. The church must maintain the proper balance of both honoring authorities and advocating for their limitations in spiritual matters.

---

[28] Thomas R. Schreiner, *1, 2 Peter, Jude*, The New American Commentary 37 (B&H, 2003), 134.

PART 2

The Christ and Nicaea

CHAPTER 3

"Light from Light, True God from True God": The Eternal Identity of the Son

[We believe] in one Lord, Jesus Christ, the Son of God, begotten from the Father, the only begotten—that is, from the substance of the Father, God from God, Light from Light, true God from true God, begotten, not made, *consubstantial* with the Father, "through whom all things came to be" (John 1:3), both the things in heaven and the things on earth.

—The Nicene Creed (325)

He is the radiance of the glory of God and
the exact imprint of his nature.

—Hebrews 1:3 (ESV)

Thinking Nicenely Today: The Nicene Creed provides essential theological and trinitarian grammar to the Christian church. The creed's longest article (section 2) focuses on the Son. The first part of the Christological article affirms that the Son is eternally from the Father and possesses the same nature as the Father. Whatever the Father is in terms of nature, so too is the Son.

I (Shawn) remember hearing the Nicene Creed read aloud for the first time in seminary class and thinking, What in the world is this? The language, the grammar, the concepts, and the cadence seemed so foreign to me. Years later, after working through Christology during seminary studies and in the early years of my pastoral ministry, I recognized that my articulation of the divinity of the Son was non-Nicene. To teach and disciple well in the local church, we must carefully articulate the divinity of the eternal Son according to Nicaea.

In chapters 3 and 4, we explore the theological message of the lengthiest article in the Nicene Creed: the doctrine of the Son. In this chapter, we look at the eternal Son within God's life before the incarnation; in chapter 4, we consider this same Son as he became flesh and ascended to glory.[1] The Nicene Creed gives us proper biblical coordinates for a faithful articulation of Christ as the divine Son: "God from God, Light from Light, true God from true God, begotten, not made, [and] *consubstantial* (of the same substance) with the Father." The Nicene Creed is scriptural, and we are convinced it should serve as a basic theological orientation for all Christians everywhere. While the creed does not solve every theological problem, it does serve as the theological first principles of Christian belief. The creed guides and aids, not replaces, our

[1] See John Anthony McGuckin, ed., *We Believe in One Lord Jesus Christ*, Ancient Christian Doctrine 2 (IVP Academic, 2009); Mark J. Edwards, ed., *We Believe in the Crucified and Risen Lord*, Ancient Christian Doctrine 3 (IVP Academic, 2009).

reading of Scripture. However, jettisoning the creed is irresponsible and disorients us from its biblical clarity about our Lord and Savior.

A Nicene Christology Part I: The Eternal Origin and Life of the Son

Eternal Generation of the Son: What Is It?

Before the events of Nicaea in 325, Alexander of Alexandria (c. 250–326/8) preached a sermon on the unity of God. Arius was reportedly in the audience. In his response to this sermon, Arius comments: "If . . . the Father begat the Son, he that was begotten had a beginning of existence; and from this, it is evident, that there was a time when the Son was not in being. It, therefore, necessarily follows that he had his existence from nothing."[2] Arius further explains that the Son is neither eternal himself nor coeternal with the Father but was generated before the creation of all things.[3] While subsequent theologians did not preserve Arius's theology in any official form, and critics used the term "Arianism" broadly to label someone a "heretic," eternal generation was the central debate that later prompted the Nicene decree and the so-called Arian controversy. As we highlighted in chapter 1, the debate was less about the Son's divinity and more about his eternal generation.

At the core of the debate was how to best understand the Son's relation to the Father as "begotten and not made." To this end,

[2] Socrates, *Eccl. Hist.* 1.5.

[3] Arius, *Letter to Alexander* 4; English translation used: Andrew Radde-Gallwitz, ed., "Arius, *Letters to Eusebius of Nicomedia and Alexander of Alexandria,*" in *God*, trans. Mark DelCogliano, vol. 1, The Cambridge Edition of Early Christian Writings (Cambridge University Press, 2017), 109–13.

the church developed the language "eternal generation of the Son." This phrase may not be a part of your everyday vocabulary, but it is vital to understanding trinitarian relations and the specific eternal relationship between the Father and the Son. The eternal generation of the Son idea unpacks what we believe and profess about God the Son as gleaned from Scripture:

> Eternal generation is the eternal act of the Father *ad intra* (that is, within the life of God without relation to anything created) to originate the person of the Son to possess the same, undivided divine substance.

We take our cue from theologian John Webster, who defines this concept as follows: "Eternal generation is the personal and eternal act of God the Father whereby he is the origin of the personal subsistence of God the Son, so communicating to the Son the one undivided divine essence."[4] Take a moment to consider our definition and its implications. Eternal generation does not insinuate that the Son was created by the Father, nor that the Son is inferior to the Father. The Gospel of John repeatedly signifies the mutual equality of the Father and Son (see John 5:18). John and numerous other New Testament texts distinguish the Son as not the Father yet equal to him in divinity. This is why the Nicene Creed eventually anathematized the Arian phrase: "There was a *time* when he [i.e., the Son] was not." If the Son is not eternally generated, then the Son ranks among the created beings and not in the eternal divine life. As we have explored already, this notion does injustice to the biblical text and the early witness of the worshipping church.

---

[4] John Webster, *God Without Measure: Working Papers in Christian Theology, Volume I: God and the Works of God*, T&T Clark Theology (Bloomsbury, 2016), 30.

Furthermore, if the Son is not eternally generated and is instead a creature, then several theological ramifications emerge. Consider the breakdown in the doctrine of God if Arius's ideas are correct:

1. Divine Aseity: Divine aseity describes God existing in himself for life and sustenance. God is not dependent on anything outside of his life for sustenance. According to Webster, "God is from himself, and from himself God gives himself . . . Aseity is life: God's life *from* and therefore *in* himself."[5] If the Son is not eternally generated, then God is not *a se* (from self), and instead God *becomes* self-sustainable only after the Son is finally brought forth from the Father.
2. Divine Immutability: Divine immutability means God is unchangeable in what constitutes God. God cannot and need not change, even by divine decree, to somehow alter himself. Thus, God is unchangeable and completely perfect (since to change would imply that God is imperfect now and can move toward perfection, or vice versa).[6] If the Son is not eternally generated, then God is not immutable, and God *becomes* Father and Son at that moment when the Son is brought forth.
3. Divine Simplicity: Divine simplicity does not refer to God being simple to understand, but to the compositional makeup of God. God is not the sum of all his parts (i.e., composite) but is all of his properties eternally and

[5] Webster, *God and the Works of God*, 19.

[6] See Thomas G. Weinandy, *Does God Change? The Word's Becoming in the Incarnation*, Studies in Historical Theology (St. Bede's, 2002); Ronni Kurtz, *No Shadow of Turning: Divine Immutability and the Economy of Redemption*, Reformed Exegetical Doctrinal Studies (Mentor, 2022).

> without division.[7] If the Son is not eternally generated, then God is not simple, since when the Son is brought forth God's composition is adjusted by being joined to a non-eternal being.

If the Son is generated from the Father, then the Son possesses all the properties of the Father, save from being the Father (i.e., consubstantiality or *homoousios*). If Arius is correct, then he does not.

Athanasius of Alexandria can help us understand the logical and biblical inconsistences in dismissing eternal generation. In *On the Council of Nicaea* (*de Decretis*), Athanasius associated the Son's eternal generation with God's eternal Fatherhood.[8] He reasoned that if there was a moment when the Son was not, then there was also a moment when the Father was not. Athanasius quotes a portion of Arius's *Thalia*: "Not always Father, not always Son. The Son was not before his generation . . . God has not always been Father of the Son. But when the Son came to be and was created, then it was that God was called his Father."[9] Whereas human fathers *become* fathers when their children are born, Athanasius remarked, "God, who exists forever, is forever Father of the Son."[10] Therefore, denying the eternal generation of the Son impacts both the eternality of God the Father and the mutability of the eternal God becoming Father and Son. Eternal

---

[7] See Steven J. Duby, *Divine Simplicity: A Dogmatic Account*, Studies in Systematic Theology 30 (T&T Clark, 2015).

[8] Amy Brown Hughes and Shawn J. Wilhite, "The Beginnings of a Pro-Nicene Trinitarian Vision: Athanasius of Alexandria on the Activity of the Son and the Spirit," in *On Classical Trinitarianism: Retrieving the Nicene Doctrine of the Triune God*, ed. Matthew Barrett (IVP Academic, 2024), 38–66.

[9] Athanasius, *De decretis* 6.

[10] Athanasius, 12.

generation is not just "ivory tower" speculation; it is essential biblical reasoning.

In the aftermath of Nicaea, affirmation of the eternal generation of the Son theologically defined Nicene Christianity. Gregory of Nyssa (c. 335–394), one of the three Cappadocian Fathers of the mid- to late fourth century, argued that there is no time interval between the Son's nonexistence and the Son's generation: "The generation of the Son is not within time, any more than the creation was before time. It is utterly wrong to introduce division into an order of existence that admits no separation and to interpolate an interval of time into the creative cause of the universe by asserting that there was a time when the author of existence did not exist."[11] The eternal generation of the Son further insinuates: (1) that no amount of temporal distinction exists between the origin of God and the origin of the Son, (2) that the eternality of the Son necessitates the eternality of the Father, and (3) that the titles "Son" and "Father" correspond to eternal and immutable appellations. When was the Son brought forth?—As long as God the Father has existed. The Father begetting the Son is an eternal act. As long as the Father has existed, so too have the Son and Spirit, and to exist "before the ages" is to exist before the creation of time (see 1 Cor 2:7).

An X from X Christology

Before you think algebra has something to do with Nicaea, let us refer you to one of the earliest recorded hymns in the Christian tradition. The church sang *Phos Hilaron*, or "Hail, Gladdening Light," to herald the light of God in trinitarian worship. The hymn has

---

[11] Gregory of Nyssa, *Against Eunomius* 1.26.

three structural parts: (1) the Son as the "gladdening Light," (2) the radiance that emanates from the trinitarian persons, and (3) the praise of the Son, who is light and life:

Hail, gladdening Light, of his pure glory poured
Who is the immortal Father, heavenly, blest,
Holiest of Holies, Jesus Christ our Lord!
Now we are at the sun's hour of rest,
The lights of evening round us shine,
We hymn the Father, Son, and Holy Spirit divine!
Worthiest art thou at all times to be sung
With undefined tongue,
Son of our God, giver of life, alone:
Therefore, in all the world the glories, Lord, they own.[12]

By singing this hymn, the church expresses the eternal light as the center of trinitarian praise and calls humanity to experience the Light of God for life.[13]

The phrase *X from X* refers to creedal statements describing the personhood and eternal nature of God subsisting in both the Father and the Son.[14] In the *X from X* framework, the same term is used on either side of a preposition ("from" or "of"). The Nicene Creed uses

---

[12] For more on the origins and textual traditions of this hymn, see Petros Vassiliadis, "From the Pauline Collection to *Phos Hilaron* of Cappadocia," *St Vladimir's Theological Quarterly* 56, no. 1 (2012): 5–16.

[13] For more on early Christian hymnody, see Andrew B. McGowan, *Ancient Christian Worship: Early Church Practices in Social, Historical, and Theological Perspective* (Baker Academic, 2014) and Brian P. Dunkle, SJ, *Enchantment and Creed in the Hymns of Ambrose of Milan*, Oxford Early Christian Studies (Oxford University Press, 2016).

[14] For more on the use of *X from X* language in pro-Nicene thought, see Michel René Barnes, *The Power of God: Δύναμις in Gregory of Nyssa's Trinitarian Theology* (Catholic University of America Press, 2001).

three descriptions of the Son: "God from God, Light from Light, true God from true God." These are truly earth-shattering affirmations. They are also immensely devotional, inspiring reverential awe in those who confess the creed. In the *X from X* (or *X of X*) framework, we see three implications for the relationship between the Son and the Father:

1. Origin of subsistence: God the Son receives his very essence from God the Father
2. Sameness of substance/nature: what the Father is, so is the Son; what the Son is, so is the Father
3. No distinction between persons: the distinction between Father and Son is solely discerned in the eternal procession (*begetting*) and not the eternal essence

The first *X* is the Son, and the second *X* is the Father; because the *X* term ("God," "Light," or "True God") remains the same in each statement, and the focal point is the essence of God rather than a distinction between the trinitarian persons. Thus, Christology produced from an *X of X* framework assumes the Son is of the Father and that what the Father is in essence, so too is the Son. As the Father is God, light, and true God, so is the Son.

The Son is "Light from Light" because he possesses the same substance (*homoousion*) of the Father and radiates the Father's eminence. The Son is the "light" that has come into the world (John 1:9; 8:12). Augustine highlights how there is one light, and yet the Father, Son, and Spirit are each all light: "For the sun also is a light, but it is corporeal; and the spiritual creature is also light, but it is not unchangeable. The Father, therefore, is light, the Son is light, and the Holy Spirit is light; but together not three lights, but one light."[15] God as light is partially analogous to the sun giving off light, as Athanasius describes:

---

[15] Augustine, *De Trinitate* 7.6.

> We see that the radiance from the sun is integral to it and that the substance of the sun is not divided or diminished, but its substance is entire, and its radiance perfect and entire, and the radiance does not diminish the substance of the light but is as it were a genuine offspring from it. Thus, we see that the Son is begotten not from without but from the Father and that Father remains entire, while the "stamp of his substance" (Heb 1:3) exists always and preserves the likeness and image without alteration.[16]

As the sun and light are integral to one another without division, the Son is the radiant light of the Father. This light of God enlightens others because the Father and Son equally possess this light. When people behold the Son, they too behold the radiance of the Father, because the Father and the Son are one (John 10:30).

Basil the Great of Caesarea, in *Letter* 52, offers a basic scriptural account of the creed to "prove . . . the meaning of the Fathers." He associates "light from light" with "of the same substance":

> For after the assertions, "light from light," "begotten of the Father's substance, not made," they [the fathers at the Council] added the phrase "of the same substance." In this they showed that the meaning attached to "light" when applied to the Father, holds good when applied to the Son. The very notion of light makes impossible any difference between one true light and another. Then, since the Father is unoriginated light and the Son is begotten light, but each is light, the Fathers were right to use the term "of the same substance," in order to establish the equal dignity of their nature.[17]

---

[16] Athanasius, *c. Ar.* 2.33.

[17] Basil of Caesarea, *Letter* 52.2.

In "Light from Light," Basil reads the eternal begetting of the Son and the sameness of nature between Father and Son.

Begotten from and Consubstantial with the Father

The words "begotten" and "consubstantial" are rarely used in sermons or Sunday school lessons. The terms, admittedly, are difficult to understand. However, the theological grammar of the early church must shape our vocabulary in the modern church so we can better understand the Son's relationship to the Father. The word "begotten" and its derivatives appear three times in the Nicene Creed. The language speaks to the nature of the Son ("begotten of the Father") and to relations of origin ("begotten not made"). The creedal line defines "only begotten" as "of the essence of the Father." To be begotten is to derive one's origin from the Father, possess the same nature as the Father, and be altogether distinct from creation and the created order. Most notable to this part of the creedal statement, to be begotten is *not* to be created. The Son's eternal relation of origin is as the "only begotten" Son. This exclusive title signifies the Son's sameness and shared nature with the Father.

Consubstantial (*homoousion*) is a deeply ingrained and necessary theological term in Christian grammar. It conveys that the Son has the same substance as the Father. Thomas Weinandy argues that *homoousios* is "historically and doctrinally, the most important word and notion within trinitarian and Christological dogma."[18] *Homoousion* describes the Son's sameness with the Father. The term "substance" (*ousia*) occurs three times in the creed:

---

[18] Thomas G. Weinandy, "The Doctrinal Significance of the Councils of Nicaea, Ephesus, and Chalcedon," in *The Oxford Handbook of Christology*, ed. Francesca Aran Murphy (Oxford University Press, 2015), 555.

1. The only begotten Son is "from the substance (*ousias*) of the Father."
2. The Father and the Son are consubstantial (*homoousion*).
3. The anathematized view of the Son is as distinct in *hypostasis* or *ousia*.

Sara Parvis explains why the Nicene Creed and in particular the term *homoousios* struggled to catch on in the years following 325. Whereas *homoousios* appears in the 381 Constantinople Creed, *ousias* does not. In the decades surrounding Nicaea, usage of these terms was contested. Parvis observes, "The Nicene Creed, including the term *homoousios*, was first sidelined, and then, from 357 to 360, officially replaced across the whole empire, with public use of *homoousios* specifically banned in 360."[19] The Nicene framers sought to express a biblical idea using language that was not yet developed or theologically tested. Though "consubstantial" (*homoousion*) became a necessary term within Christian theology, the authors of the creed did not realize how it would be applied, especially as we understand it now.[20] Lewis Ayres rightly notes, "It is not at all clear that at Nicaea the term *homoousios* was understood to be the technical focus of the creed."[21] *Homoousios* was "originally chosen for polemical purposes and without any defense," and a "well-established

[19] Sara Parvis, "The Reception of Nicaea and *Homoousios* to 360," in *The Cambridge Companion to the Council of Nicaea*, ed. Young Richard Kim, Cambridge Companions to Religion (Cambridge University Press, 2021), 225.

[20] David M. Gwynn, "Reconstructing the Council of Nicaea," in *The Cambridge Companion to the Council of Nicaea*, ed. Young Richard Kim, Cambridge Companions to Religion (Cambridge University Press, 2021), 101.

[21] Ayres, *Nicaea and Its Legacy*, 93.

theological meaning was gradually identified as a key marker of pro-Nicene orthodoxy."[22]

Homoousios refers to the fact that the Son is proper to the Father's nature, so that the Son possesses all that belongs to the Father equally and without division. Whatever language we use to describe the eternal life of God, in terms of nature, we may use to describe the Son. God the Father is immutable; therefore, God the Son is immutable; the Father is impassible; therefore, the Son is impassible. The Son cannot be distinguished from the Father in terms of nature because the Son is *homoousion* with the Father. Athanasius used the term *homoousios* himself once before 353 (*c. Ar.* 2.9) and defends Nicaea's use of "from the substance of the Father" and *homoousios* in *de Decretis* 19–24. He agrees with the Council's usage because (1) the Son's generation from the Father is different from human generation, (2) the Son is entirely like (*homoios*) the Father, (3) the Son's essence is inseparable from the Father's essence, and (4) the Father and Son are one (i.e., the Father is in the Son and the Son is in the Father). Athanasius states: "The council, understanding all this [i.e., these four reasons], aptly wrote 'one in essence' (*homoousion*)."[23]

The Eternal Son as an Agent of Creation

The Father, Son, and Spirit each play an active role in creation. Before the incarnation or any manifestation of the Son in creation, the Son was the agent of the created world, in that the Father created the world through the Son in the Spirit. The creedal explanation

---

[22] Lewis Ayres, "Athanasius' Initial Defense of the Term Homoousios: Rereading the *De Decretis*," *Journal of Early Christian Studies* 12, no. 3 (fall 2004): 339.

[23] *de Decretis* 20.

reflects several Scriptures (John 1:3, 10; 1 Cor 8:6; Col 1:16; Heb 1:2, 10). God the Father *alone* is not Creator, but the Father is the Creator, the Son is the Creator, *and* the Spirit is the Creator (Gen 1:2; Job 26:13; 34:14–15; Ps 33:6; Isa 40:12–13).[24]

In *Against the Arians*, Athanasius links creation directly to the eternal generation of the Son: "The Word of God was not made for us; rather, we were made for him, and 'in him all things were created' (Col 1:15). Nor is it true that because of our weakness he, the strong, was brought into being by the Father, who then existed alone, in order that he might fashion us through him as by an instrument. Nothing could be further from the truth."[25] The Son's creative activity is not out of any need. His identity as Creator requires us to affirm the aseity of the Father and the Son—God is self-sufficient in himself. Athanasius then proceeds with a second line of reasoning about the Son's eternal relationship with the Father: The Son has *always* been with the Father, in the same way that light and radiance relate. Irrespective of the created realm being brought forth, the Son has always been with the Father.[26] The Son's eternal existence with the Father is a necessary precursor to

---

[24] In *c.* ninth century, a hymn was composed, entitled "Veni Creator Spiritus" ("Come, Creator Spirit"). This trinitarian hymn, which centers the Spirit, has been sung by Catholic and Protestant Christians. For more on a theology of the Spirit, see Raniero Cantalamessa, *Come, Creator Spirit: Meditations on the* Veni Creator (Liturgical Press, 2003); Fred Sanders, *The Holy Spirit: An Introduction*, Short Studies in Systematic Theology (Crossway, 2023).

[25] Athanasius, *c. Ar.* 2.31.

[26] Athanasius, *c. Ar.* 2.31: "For even if God had decided not to make created things, still the Word would have been 'with God' nonetheless, and the Father in him, while created things could not have come into being without the Word. . . . The Word of God is creator and maker, and he is the Father's very will."

describing the Son as Creator. The Son is always with God and is the creative agent of the Father's creative activity.

Hilary of Poitiers (c. 310–367) named the Son as Creator in *De Trinitate* and offered two premises: (1) the Son as Creator distinguishes himself from creation, and (2) the Son as Creator precedes all creation. In Book 12, Hilary noted, "He [the Son] is our Creator, the Creator of the whole heavenly army."[27] He posed a question to affirm the Son as Creator in the apostolic and evangelical faith:

> Since all of these texts refer to the Son, through whom everything has been made and are to be understood in accordance with the apostolic and evangelical faith, how shall He be made equal to these very creatures whom He has made and be given a name common to all of them?[28]

Because creation is subject to decay, the Son cannot be created, since he cannot be subject to corruption. In 4.16–20, Hilary quotes several Scriptures, including 1 Cor 8:6 and selected verses from Genesis 1, to note that God creates and is not with an inferior being.[29]

---

[27] Hilary of Poitiers, *De Trinitate* 12.4. In 5.5 too, Hilary describes the Son: "He is God, He is the Creator, He is the Son of God, He can do all things."

[28] Hilary of Poitiers, *De Trinitate* 12.5.

[29] Hilary of Poitiers, *De Trinitate* 4.16: "Consequently, the God from whom are all things says that they are to be made, and the God through whom are all things makes them, and the same name is applied equally in the designation of him who commands and for the work of Him who carries it out. If you will dare to claim that the Son is not referred to when it is stated, 'And God made it' (Gen 1:1–2:3), what will be your attitude to where it is said, 'All things were made through Him' (John 1:3), and those words, 'And our one Lord, Jesus Christ, through whom are all things' (1 Cor 8:6) and that statement, 'He spoke and they were made' (Ps 33:9)?"

Biblical Connections

There is eternal significance in affirming the eternal generation of the Son. The doctrine of God is at stake when we disrupt the eternality of any member of the Trinity. While the Scripture does not explicate a full-orbed theology of divine relations, every vital building block exists in the text. While the term and concept of *homoousias* emerged untested in 325, it came to be accepted as the best way to express what we confess about the divinity of Christ. Since the Son is of the same substance as the Father, we can trust what he says and experience his grace for us. With this in mind, we briefly look at John 15.

Throughout John's gospel narrative, Jesus declares his unity with the Father. He proclaims that he and the Father are one in John 10:30. Then, in John 15 (ESV), he encourages his disciples to "abide," or "remain," in him and his love. This could be interpreted as merely sentimental if our interpretation was not based on the ontological reality that the Father and Son are one. To remain in the Son's love is to necessarily abide in the love of God the Father. Jesus commands in verses 9 and 10: "As the Father has loved me, I have also loved you. Remain in my love. If you keep my commands you will remain in my love, just as I have kept my Father's commands and remain in his love." This is no mere pietistic emotionalism. Jesus's command to abide rests on the assurance that he alone is the basis of our abiding.

To "remain" in the love of Christ is both a passive and active act. It is passive because we have received the love of God in Christ, and through his work alone, we "remain" secure in the love of God. It is active because we are called to faithfully walk in the divine love extended to us by the Son. Thus, to cohere to the person and work of Christ is to be bound to God's very life and love.

Colin Kruse concludes, "While there are some differences, it still remains an immense privilege for disciples of Jesus to be brought into the community of love that exists between the Father and the Son."[30] In the grace of the incarnation, we are able to deeply experience divine love. Augustine observed, "Accordingly, therefore, we can correctly say that, although human nature doesn't belong to God's nature, nonetheless human nature belongs through grace to the person of the only-begotten Son of God, and so great is the grace that none is greater, and unquestionably none is equal."[31] We experience divine love based on divine initiative and divine invitation. That invitation is the incarnation. The Son's divinity contains all the rich storehouses of God's love precisely because he is one in essence with the Father.

Conclusion

We invite Christians into a pro-Nicene theological framework and present a sampling of theological reasoning from fourth-century theologians to strengthen our own. The Son is "God from God, Light from Light, True God from True God, begotten, not made, [and] consubstantial with the Father"—this is biblical Christology. To affirm otherwise is not only detrimental to doctrine, but to the Christian life. The Nicene Creed begins the Christological article by offering propositional statements

---

[30] Colin G. Kruse, *John: An Introduction and Commentary*, Tyndale New Testament Commentaries 4 (IVP Academic, 2003), 315.

[31] *Io. eu. tr.* 82.4 in Edmund Hill, trans., *Saint Augustine: Homilies on the Gospel of John 41–124*, The Works of Saint Augustine: A Translation for the 21st Century 13 (New City Press, 2020), 295.

demarcating the Son's eternal divine life. If you have never considered the cosmic weight of the Son's divinity, the creed guides you toward this biblical confession. The creed offers us a scriptural view of God that explodes our Christian imagination, beckoning us to step inside the eternal divine life and marvel at the wonder of God's triune majesty.

CHAPTER 4

"He Became Human . . . and Ascended into the Heavens": Christ's Humility and Exaltation

[He] became human. For us, he was crucified under Pontius Pilate, suffered, was buried, and rose on the third day according to the Scriptures. [He] ascended into the heavens, is seated at the right hand of the Father, and is coming again with glory "to judge the living and the dead" (2 Tim 4:1; 1 Pet 4:5), whose kingdom will have no end.

—The Niceno-Constantinople Creed (381)

But [he] emptied himself, by taking the form of a servant, being born in the likeness of men. And being found in human form, he humbled himself by becoming obedient to the point of death, even death on a cross.

—Philippians 2:7–8 (ESV)

Thinking Nicenely Today: Though the church provided further clarity after Nicaea regarding the two natures of the Son, the Council of Nicaea addressed the Son as eternal and as a human. Christians must take seriously the tension of Christ's humanity in light of his divinity. The vital ministry of the church stands or falls based on her affirmation of Christ's full humanity.

In our experience, Christians tend to be familiar with the topics of this chapter. As the Apostles' Creed insists, the Lord Jesus Christ was born of a virgin, lived, suffered, was crucified and died, was buried, and resurrected; he ascended into the heavens, sat down at the Father's right hand, and will return in glory. What a glorious and cosmos-altering truth! Have you considered the significance of God the Son taking on flesh for your sake? We will explore the beauty of salvation and sanctification in later chapters, but we invite you to first pause and dwell on your Lord, who added to himself a human nature so that we would not only be redeemed but welcomed into the divine life. The humanity of the Son is itself the divine invitation welcoming us into the life of the triune God.

This chapter includes two distinct sections about the life of the Son. Our understanding of the life of the Son can be spread over three movements: the Son's (1) eternal divine life; (2) humiliation and incarnation; and (3) ascension, exaltation, and eventual return. Chapter 3 covered the first movement, and this chapter will consider the second and third. If we get the divine life of Christ wrong, we jettison the biblical doctrine of God. But if we confound the humanity of Christ, we lose the gospel altogether. From a Nicene perspective, the two discussions are inseparable and necessary for our proper understanding of both the biblical revelation and the gospel message.

A Nicene Christology Part II: The Humiliation and Incarnation

Salvation as the Reason for the Incarnation

After addressing the eternal identity of the Son, the Nicene Creed reveals *why* this same Son was made incarnate: for us and for our salvation. Let us ponder this together for a moment: The eternal Son descended to creation to provide salvation for humanity. The Son was made flesh for us. The old Charles Wesley hymn resonates this truth: "And can it be that I should gain / An int'rest in the Savior's blood? / Died He for me, who caused His pain? / For me, who Him to death pursued? / Amazing love! how can it be / That Thou, my God, shouldst die for me?"[1] Our confession of Christ's incarnation is not an abstraction; it is both piercingly personal and cosmically consequential.

To properly contemplate the Son's death, we must grasp the earthly life of the incarnate Son. His descent to become human and the virgin birth by Mary were just as necessary to our salvation as his suffering, death, burial, and resurrection. The entire incarnational life of the Son is for us and for our salvation. Both Athanasius and Augustine consider the soteriological implications of the incarnation.

Athanasius argued that the Son became human to restore humanity. The Son is like the Father in every way, save from being the Father. The Son came "to renew the human being made according to himself and to find him, as one lost, through the forgiveness of sins, as he says in the Gospels, 'I came to seek and

[1] Charles Wesley, "And Can It Be?" (1738), public domain.

to save the lost.'"[2] In Luke 19:10, human salvation is the focal reason the Son became incarnate. Athanasius connects the incarnation to the knowledge and presence of God filling the entire space of the created realm: "Properly, therefore, the Word of God took a body and used a human instrument, in order to give life to the body and in order that, just as he is known in creation by his works, so also he might act in a human being, and show himself everywhere, leaving nothing barren of his divinity and knowledge." The Word of God gives life to the human body and is made known to creation. In this way, God occupies both heaven and the created realm, filling both spheres with his presence. As Athanasius notes, the incarnation fulfills this language from Isa 11:9: "The whole earth was filled with the knowledge of God."[3] For Athanasius, the incarnation intersects total human transformation with cosmic reconciliation.

Several years after Athanasius, Augustine uses a medicinal metaphor to describe salvation:

> The Son of God then assumed a human nature and bore patiently therein all human misery. The healing power of this medicine for men is beyond all comprehension. For, what pride can be cured, if it is not cured by the humility of the Son of God? What avarice can be cured, if it is not cured by the poverty of the Son of God? What anger can be cured, if it is not cured by the patience of the Son of God? What ungodliness can be cured, if it is not cured by the charity of the Son of God? Finally, what want of

---

[2] Athanasius, *On the Incarnation* 14. English translation: John Behr, trans., *Saint Athanasius: On the Incarnation*, Popular Patristics Series 44a (St. Vladimir's Seminary Press, 2011).

[3] Athanasius, *On the Incarnation* 45.

> courage can be cured, if it is not cured by the resurrection of the body?[4]

As a spiritual cure, the Son's lived life heals the polarity of human ailments. If pride, the Son's humility heals. If greediness, the Son's poverty heals. If anger, the Son's patience heals. If cowardice, the Son's resurrection heals. In these examples, the Son's lived life saves humanity. Saint Gregory of Nazianzus's dictum, more well-known than Augustine's statement, is like it: "For that which is not assumed is not healed, that which is united to God is being saved."[5] The sixth ecumenical council of the church, the Third Council of Constantinople (680–681) also affirmed this Christological soteriology: "For what was not assumed by him is not saved."[6]

The Eternal Son Made Flesh

Admittedly, it is not easy to fathom an eternal being who decides to willingly take on mortality in the manner described in the New Testament. History is filled with stories and myths of gods taking a human form or acting in human ways, but the point is almost never to denigrate their god-ness. The god maintains divine rights and even uses power indiscriminately. In many stories, from ancient Greek mythology to modern Marvel movies, so-called gods act more like petulant children with superhuman abilities.

---

[4] Augustine, *The Christian Combat* 11. English translation: Robert P. Russel, trans. *Saint Augustine: Christian Instruction; Admonition and Grace; The Christian Combat; Faith, Hope and Charity*, FC 2 (Catholic University of America Press, 1947), 309–53.

[5] *Ep.* 101.5.

[6] E. Schwartz, ed., *Acta conciliorum oecumenicorum* II, 2, 1–2, doc. 4, 76.

This is, of course, not what Christians believe when we confess the Son made flesh. When the Son became human, he retained his entire divinity. As Paul describes in Phil 2:7, the Son "empties himself" by "assuming the form of a servant, taking on the likeness of humanity." The "emptying" is not a divesting of glory, but his assumption of humanity. Now, the eternal Son made flesh is of two natures! Of course, the Nicene Creed does not answer every Christological question, but it provides the theological framework and doxological key we need to begin understanding the mystery of the incarnation.

So, how does the eternal Son, coeternal and consubstantial with the Father, enter creation's fray and become human? Additionally, how does the Son become human without changing (losing his *immutability*) or affecting (losing his *impassibility)* the eternal life of God? In his second recorded letter to Nestorius, Cyril of Alexandria reflected on Christology and the Nicene Creed.[7] According to Mark Smith, "Cyril sought to give an explicit and cogent theological rationale for how the Nicene Creed should be interpreted."[8] Cyril called the Nicene Council "the holy and great council," and encouraged Nestorius to "follow these words [i.e., a summary of its Christological article] and teaching, keeping in mind what having been 'made flesh' means."[9] Ultimately, how the two natures relate to one another in the single Son is an ineffable mystery. Cyril describes: "The differences of the natures are not

[7] While we refrain from exploring Cyril's controversy with Nestorius in the early fifth century, his *Second Letter to Nestorius* has become a standard source for rightly reading the Nicene Creed.

[8] Mark S. Smith, *The Idea of Nicaea in the Early Church Councils, AD 431–451*, OECS (Oxford University Press, 2019), 49.

[9] Cyril of Alexandria, *ep.* 4.3. English translation: John I. McEnerney, trans., *St. Cyril of Alexandria: Letters 1–50*, The Fathers of the Church 76 (Catholic University of America Press, 1987).

destroyed through the union, but rather the divinity and humanity formed for us one Lord Jesus Christ and one Son through the incomprehensible and ineffable combination to a unity."[10]

Theologians describe this mystery as the *hypostatic union*, the mysterious union of two natures in the eternal Word made flesh. When the Son became human, the divine nature remained immutable and encountered what is human. Though the natures are diametrically different, the two natures are united in the one Son. Cyril provides two categories of what this union cannot mean: neither was the divine nature "altered when he became flesh," nor was the Word "a complete man of soul and body," forgoing what is divine.[11] The eternal Son united with what is human *hypostatically*, so that the two natures, being wholistically different in every way, are mysteriously joined together in the one Lord Jesus Christ.[12]

Theologians offer another term to describe how the two natures manifest in the one Son: *communicatio idiomatum* ("communication of idioms" or "communication of properties"). As Steven Duby relates, the *communicatio idiomatum* is "the communication or sharing of the properties of the two natures in the one person of Christ."[13] Oliver Crisp warns that we must avoid "predicating attributes of one nature that properly belong to the other nature in the hypostatic union, without transference of properties between the natures and without confusing or commingling the two natures of Christ."[14] The Scriptures use both "human" qualities to describe the eternal Word and "divine" qualities to

---

[10] *ep.* 4.3.

[11] *ep.* 4.3.

[12] *ep.* 4.3.

[13] Steven J. Duby, *Jesus and the God of Classical Theism: Biblical Christology in Light of the Doctrine of God* (Baker Academic, 2022), 166.

[14] Oliver D. Crisp, *Divinity and Humanity: The Incarnation Reconsidered* (Cambridge University Press, 2007), 7–8.

describe the incarnate Word. The incarnation of the Son permits us to attribute both properties, divine and human, to the Lord Jesus Christ. In the incarnation, the Son did not cease being divine, but he is now fully divine and human. Cyril of Alexandria asserts, "Therefore, there is one Lord Jesus Christ, the very Only-Begotten Word of the Father made man, who did not relinquish being what he was, for he remained God in his humanity."[15] The Son remained God while also assuming humanity. The "emptying" recorded in Philippians 2 was not a divestment of divinity but a condescension of the eternal God to become human. The Son assumed humanity with his full divinity. The Son is both born of a virgin and eternally begotten; he is both human and remains what he was, a single person, though he possesses two different natures. This reality remains one of the great mysteries of the Christian faith.

After it was confessed in the creed, this great mystery gained clarity in the subsequent decades and into the fifth century. The "Faith of the 318" (the Council of Nicaea) and "Faith of the 150" (the Council of Constantinople in 381) serve as a theological anchor to the Christological vision of the Council of Chalcedon (451). The parliamentary notes of session two at Chalcedon record that they began with a recitation of the two creeds: "We wish you to know that the most divine and pious master of the world and we ourselves preserve the orthodox faith handed down by the 318, by the 150, and by the other holy and glorious fathers, and believe in accordance with it."[16] We provide selected portions of the Chalcedonian definition of the Son:

---

[15] Cyril of Alexandria, *ep.* 55.22.

[16] Session II.2. *The Acts of the Council of Chalcedon: Translated with an Introduction and Notes*, vol. 2, Translated Texts for Historians 45 (Liverpool University Press, 2005), 10.

> Following, therefore, the holy fathers, we all in harmony teach confession of one and the same Son our Lord Jesus Christ, the same perfect in Godhead and the same perfect in manhood, truly God and the same truly man . . .
>
> . . . the same consubstantial with us in respect of the manhood, like us in all things apart from sin, begotten from the Father before the ages in respect of the Godhead, and the same consubstantial with us in respect of the manhood, like us in all things apart from sin . . .
>
> . . . one and the same Christ, Son, Lord, Only-begotten, acknowledged in two natures without confusion, change, division, or separation (the difference of the natures being in no way destroyed by the union, but rather the distinctive character of each nature being preserved and coming together into one person and one hypostasis) . . . [17]

The Lord Jesus Christ became flesh and assumed an additional nature without affecting the eternal nature. By confessing the *hypostatic union,* we confess the eternal Son "becomes flesh" (without sin) so that the two natures are united without confusion, change, division, or separation. What started at Nicaea and gained clarity at Constantinople blossomed into a full expression of the two natures of the Son at Chalcedon and into the sixth and seventh centuries (namely, with Maximus the Confessor).

The Suffering, Burial, and Resurrection of the Son

The remaining descriptions of the Son in the creed include more familiar historical and theological concepts. All Christians know of Jesus Christ's suffering, crucifixion, death and burial, resurrection,

[17] Session V.34. *The Acts of the Council of Chalcedon*, 2:204.

ascension, and future return. We anchor these events to the gospel declaration in 1 Corinthians 15 and other passages and offer relevant commentary by Augustine.

Each of the four Gospels concludes with a lengthy description of the Son's suffering, crucifixion under Pontius Pilate, and burial. In 1 Corinthians 15, Paul summarizes the gospel message that he preached. Interestingly, the Nicene confession includes several statements that correspond to 1 Cor 15:3–4 (ESV): "For I delivered to you as of first importance what I also received: that Christ died for our sins in accordance with the Scriptures, that he was buried, that he was raised on the third day in accordance with the Scriptures." Because the creed incorporates the statements from 1 Corinthians 15, we conclude that the Nicene Creed includes a faithful account of the Gospel of our Lord Jesus Christ. The true events recounted in Scripture are the basis for the true statements recorded in the creed.

The Nicene Creed predominantly explains these features in terse and simple phrases: "he was crucified . . . he suffered . . . [he] was buried." Its wording avoids atonement theory or concerns about passibility (i.e., the question, How is it that "he suffered"?—also known as *theopaschism*); instead, because the first part of the creed establishes the eternal Son as "true God from true God," it confirms that this same eternal Son, who has become man, has suffered.[18] Augustine combines the themes of love, God's inseparable operations, and justification in his speech about the death of the Son.[19] Christ's death is the means of our justification and reconciliation with God. Additionally, the Father offered the Son for

---

[18] For an exploration of *theopaschism* in early Christian thought, see Paul L. Gavrilyuk, *The Suffering of the Impassible God: The Dialectics of Patristic Thought*, OECS (Oxford University Press, 2004).

[19] Augustine, *De Trinitate* 13.11.15.

our salvation, not by the separation of the persons of the Trinity but by all three acting in concert with the other. The Trinity's inseparable activity and the Son's crucifixion are mysteriously linked in Christian theology.[20]

The incarnation and resurrection are necessary to salvation. Without the Son's assumption of what belongs to humanity, we have no redeemer. Without the Son's resurrection from the dead, we remain in our sins (1 Cor 15:12–19). The resurrection is the visible proof that the Son is the eternal Son of God, and it secures our salvation (Rom 4:25). The eternal Son descended from heaven to earth and then to the "lower parts of the earth" (Eph 4:8–10). The resurrection functions as the first movement of the Son back up toward the heavens.

Augustine, too, commented on the *historicity* of these events. The creedal lines assume a repetitive structure (i.e., "he suffered . . . [he] was buried . . . he arose . . . he ascended . . . he sits . . . he will come"). Augustine contended, "So, whatever took place in Christ's crucifixion, his burial, his resurrection on the third day, his ascension into heaven and his sitting at the right hand of the Father was done in such a way that Christians might live within these mysteries, which are historical facts and not merely mystical utterances."[21] The resurrection turns our sorrow and mourning into joy and gladness. No longer can death reign over humanity. Pain, sickness, cancer, and suffering no longer have the final word. Now

---

[20] For more on this topic, see Matthew Y. Emerson and Brandon D. Smith, *Beholding the Triune God: The Inseparable Work of Father, Son, and Spirit* (Crossway, 2024).

[21] Augustine, *Enchiridion* 14, 53. English translation: Bruce Harbert, trans., *Augustine of Hippo: The Augustine Catechism; the Enchiridion on Faith, Hope, and Charity*, vol. 1 of The Augustine Series (New City Press, 1999), 83.

that Christ has risen from the dead, our fears of death (though they may remain) are overshadowed and defeated (Heb 2:14–15).

A Nicene Christology Part III: The Ascension and Exaltation

The Ascension of the Son

Luke records the only historical narrative of the Son's ascension (Luke 24:50–53 and Acts 1:9–11). It was foretold in the Old Testament (Ps 110:1//Acts 2:34; Ps 68:18//Eph 4:8) and by Jesus in the New Testament (John 7:33–36; 8:21; 16:5–7). The ascension is theologically significant for several reasons; namely, it begins the rule and reign of Christ (Acts 2:33–35), signifies the supremacy of Christ above all things (Eph 1:20–22), and marks when the church receives the Spirit and the gifts of the Spirit (Eph 4:8). Mark Edwards reflects on the ascension of the Son in Patristic thought: "In retaining this clause from the earlier creeds, however, they have allotted it to a position that clearly indicates that the ascension did not bestow a new dignity on the eternal Son but revealed him for what he had always been; and that he did not bring his human element down from heaven but assumed it on earth, so that this, unlike the Godhead, is now exalted for the first time."[22] The Son in his divinity returns to where he has always been, and in his humanity enters heaven for the very first time.

Tyrannius Rufinus of Aquileia (c. 344–411) reflects on the Christological clauses of the Apostles' Creed, which often mirrors the Nicene Creed. Regarding the Son's ascension, session, and

[22] Mark J. Edwards, ed., *We Believe in the Crucified and Risen Lord*, Ancient Christian Doctrine 3 (IVP Academic, 2009), 155.

future return, Rufinus states, "These clauses, coming at the end of the article, are expressed with fitting brevity. Their affirmations are clear enough: what demands explanation is the sense in which they ought to be understood."[23] Rufinus also notes that the ascension, session, and future return require a two-nature Christology: "For unless our interpretation of 'ascend,' 'sits,' and 'will come' consorts with the dignity of the Godhead, we shall suppose them to convey a suggestion of human weakness."[24] J. N. D. Kelly comments:

> Rufinus is concerned in this passage to point out that a firm grasp of what was later to be called the doctrine of the Two Natures is essential to an understanding of the Ascension, Session, and Second Coming. If we overlook the fact that the Son eternally abides in the Father in His divine nature, we shall slip into the error of regarding Him as a mere man raised to the divine level by adoption.[25]

Athanasius reflects on Phil 2:9–10 and the exaltation of the Son in *Against the Arians* 1.37–45. Athanasius argues that the language of "humbled" and "exalted" in Philippians 2 refers to the Son by his humanity, and not to his divinity. He asks, Why does the eternal Son subsisting with a divine nature need to be exalted unless that divine nature was altered somehow? Athanasius comments:

> The term in question, "highly exalted," does not signify that the essence of the Word was exalted, for He was ever and is equal to God, but the exaltation is of the

[23] Rufinus, *Rufinus: A Commentary on the Apostles' Creed*, trans. J. N. D. Kelly, Ancient Christian Writers 20 (Newman, 1955), 31.

[24] Rufinus, 31.

[25] J. N. D. Kelly, *Rufinus: A Commentary on the Apostles' Creed*, 130.

> manhood. . . . Since then, the Word, being the Image of the Father and immortal, took the form of the servant, and as man underwent for us death in His flesh, that thereby He might offer Himself for us through death to the Father; therefore also, as man, He is said because of us and for us to be highly exalted.[26]

Of course, the incarnate Son is a single Son with two natures. However, as Athanasius describes, the Son subsisting with the nature of humanity requires the language of humility and subsequent exaltation. The Son cannot be brought low or exalted by what is divine because he is already considered the Highest.[27]

The Return and Judgment of the Son

There is no faithful gospel proclamation without the return and judgment of Christ. "Christ has died, Christ has risen, Christ will come again" is the hope-filled cry of the church. When we gather around the table of our Lord, we take bread and wine to remember both his body and blood, as well as "proclaim the Lord's death until he comes" (1 Cor 11:26). So, the return of the Lord offers hope to the believer. The Nicene Creed reminds us that correct theological confessions reflect the Christian hope of the Lord's return. The Fathers who put together the creed reflected on Scripture. The creed is not some abstract theological belief lacking scriptural affirmation—just the opposite! The "Olivet Discourse" in the Gospels (Matt 24–25; Mark 13; Luke 21) and language in 1 and 2 Thessalonians associate the Gospel of our Lord Jesus directly with

---

[26] Athanasius, *c. Ar.* 1.41.

[27] Athanasius, *c. Ar.* 1.40.

the return of the Lord. The early statements about the ascension of our Lord in Acts 1 also remind us that his physical return will parallel the ascension.

We provide structure from Cyril of Jerusalem, who instructs catechumens on the creed. Cyril offers seven twofold patterns associated with the Lord Jesus in his *Catechetical Lectures* 15.1:

1. Two advents: the coming of Christ in his birth and the coming of Christ in his glory
2. Two generations: one eternally of the Father and one finitely of the Virgin
3. Two descents: the coming of Christ as unobservable in his birth and the coming of Christ as visible in his glory
4. Two cloth coverings: first, in swaddling clothes; and second, with light as his garment (Ps 104:2)
5. Two different postures: first, the endurance of the cross, despising shame, and second; the receiving of glory being attended by a host of angels
6. Two announcements: the same announcement of "Blessed is he who comes in the name of the Lord" at both his first and his second advents (Matt 21:9; 23:39)
7. Two judgments of the Lord: first, that the Lord Jesus Christ was judged, and then his return to judge the world

Cyril explains this twofold pattern:

> We preach not one advent only of Christ, but a second also, far more glorious than the former. For the former gave a view of His patience; but the latter brings with it the crown of a divine kingdom. For all things, for the most part, are twofold in the Lord Jesus Christ; a twofold generation; one, of God, before the ages; and one, of a Virgin, at the close of the ages: His descents twofold; one, the

> unobserved, "like rain on a fleece" (Ps 72:6); and a second His open coming, which is to be.[28]

The coming of the Lord is twofold: first, his incarnation, and second, his glorious return. His return as the incarnate King of kings will usher in a new heavens and new earth where righteousness will dwell (Isa 65:17; 2 Pet 3:13; Rev 21:1). We take comfort in his return, which sustains us in our current trials and suffering. The glorious return also informs our faithful living in the present, as we witness to the lost and perishing and call the world to behold the beauty of God and trust in his salvation provided by the Son. Confession of Christ's full divinity and humanity—his entire career—as necessary for salvation is the essence of the Nicene Creed because it is the essence of the gospel message.

Biblical Connections

We return to 1 Corinthians, first chapter 15 and then chapter 11. In these chapters, Paul challenges the Corinthian church to understand the gravity of their confession, both in doctrine and practice. In chapter 15, Paul's exhortation regarding the resurrection provides a concrete expectation for believers: "Listen, I am telling you a mystery: We will not all fall asleep, but we will all be changed, in a moment, in the twinkling of an eye, at the last trumpet. For the trumpet will sound, and the dead will be raised incorruptible, and we will be changed" (1 Cor 15:51–52). On the last day, Christ will return in victory, and our corruptible bodies will become incorruptible and glorious like his. Our hope in things not seen will be made sight, and our final salvation will be accomplished. We cannot begin to comprehend what the final resurrection will entail.

[28] Cyril of Jerusalem, *Catechetical Lectures* 15.1.

Mark Taylor notes, "While Paul's language gives us a glimpse of the nature of the resurrection body, it still lies beyond our comprehension. What is clear, however, is that the essence of resurrection is the transformation of our earthly bodies."[29] Augustine declared, "When that resurrection of the body does come to pass, we shall be freed from the constraints of time and enjoy unending life in a love and security beyond description."[30]

In 1 Corinthians 11, Paul exhorted the church to practice what it preached, specifically relating to the sacrament of the Lord's Supper. The liturgy of the Lord's Supper both spiritualizes and memorializes Christ's life, death, and resurrection, and affirms the abiding hope that he will come again. The spiritual impact of the Eucharist in the life of the community cannot be underestimated. "The emphasis," according to Leon Morris, "is on the vicarious work of Christ; what happened to the body was for us. There was purpose in his suffering, a purpose of blessing for his people."[31] We advocate for a weekly observance of the Supper because we cannot have enough reminders of Christ's work for us. The incarnation of Christ is recognized every time we break the bread and take the cup in worship. We use material signs to declare the material reality of the Son taking on flesh for us and our salvation, and these material objects correspond to spiritual realities of Christ's sustaining nourishment for us. While sermons and Bible studies reinforce our

---

[29] Mark Taylor, *1 Corinthians*, The New American Commentary 28 (B&H, 2014), 405.

[30] *De fide et Symb.* 10.24 in Augustine of Hippo, "Faith and the Creed," in *On Christian Belief*, trans. Michael G. Campbell, vol. I/8, The Works of Saint Augustine: A Translation for the 21st Century (New City Press, 2005), 174.

[31] Leon Morris, *1 Corinthians: An Introduction and Commentary*, Tyndale New Testament Commentaries 7 (IVP, 1985), 158.

doctrine, the Supper uniquely reinforces our soul with the humble declaration of God's love for us in Christ.

Conclusion

The creed summarizes both the divine and human reality of the Son. There is no true gospel message apart from Christ's fundamental yet profound declaration as the incarnate Lord for our salvation. We hope the creed's content forms a more conscious role in the life of the Christian church. The Christological article beautifully summarizes the person and work of the Son. It opens up the world of the divine life of God, inviting us to enter his splendor and awesome majesty. The past two chapters provide a structure to the creed, offer scriptural proof-texts, suggest additional theological resources, and propose forms of theological reasoning for the Nicene tradition. Next, we examine how the biblical truths declared at Nicaea should shape our view of salvation, Christian life, and the church's ministry.

PART 3

The Christian and Nicaea

CHAPTER 5

"For Us Humans and for Our Salvation": The Beauty of Salvation

For us humans and for our salvation, he descended
from the heavens and became incarnate from the Holy
Spirit and the Virgin Mary, and [he] became human.
—The Niceno-Constantinople Creed (381)

In him was life, and that life was the light of
men. That light shines in the darkness, and
yet the darkness did not overcome it.
—John 1:4–5

Thinking Nicenely Today: Salvation is accomplished through the whole person and work of the eternal Son made flesh. Nicaea's scriptural, truthful claims display that the incarnation of the eternal Word is for us and our salvation. Salvation is a cosmic and beautiful event, the effects of which begin to unfold now and extend into eternity. Christ's redemption is a mystery of wonder, amazement, and beauty.

We are familiar with trophies in our society. Tokens of victory and effort in sports and spelling bees adorn our bedrooms and school hallways. One fourth-century church father, Athanasius of Alexandria, described another kind of trophy. This trophy was not a shiny medal or plaque, but a sweat-drenched, blood-soaked cross. What was to many the decisive sign of defeat eventually became the ultimate sign of victory. Jesus, in his life and crucifixion, obtained a triumph unlike any before, and his defeat of sin and Satan ushered in a new era of glory for humanity. Jesus Christ showed that he was victorious over death itself.

The beauty of the Word made flesh is the pivotal moment securing God's redemption of humanity. After Mary gave birth to the incarnate Son, the world was never the same. Romans 5:6 confirms this, saying, "For while we were still helpless, at the right time, Christ died for the ungodly." Salvation is displayed in the victory of Christ's work *for* us, as well as the beauty of Christ's work displayed *in* us. Chapter 6 focuses on the analogy of salvation and spiritual transformation, while in chapter 5 we consider the glorious nature of salvation as beautiful. Salvation is a multipronged event in Scripture, and the Fathers held that it comprised the incarnation, death and burial, resurrection, and glorification of the Son. The "trophy" of Christ is beauty itself and the basis of our salvation and transformation. The death and resurrection of the Word made flesh secured for us what no other one could: complete salvation.

The Fathers who gathered at Nicaea were concerned about many things, even beyond the creedal formulation we outline (e.g., the canons of Nicaea and the date of Easter). Though one aspect of the conversation was primarily about the Son's nature and relationship to the Father, Christian salvation is tethered to the discussion about the Son and salvation. What is needed for salvation? How does the person and work of the Son fit into the equation? If we misunderstand the Son, we will misunderstand salvation.

Athanasius of Alexandria and Gregory of Nazianzus defended the theological foundations put forth at Nicaea and extended them in the following decades of the fourth century. Specifically, Athanasius argues against Arian theology in *On the Incarnation* and *Four Discourses Against the Arians*. Gregory provides his thoughts on the subject in *The Five Theological Orations*. Both men emphasize that salvation is only possible through a Nicene understanding of the gospel, since deviating from the Son as "true God from true God" has eternal consequences.

Athanasius on the Beauty of Salvation

As a young deacon, Athanasius accompanied his bishop, Alexander, to the Council of Nicaea. Soon after the council, Athanasius was ordained bishop of Alexandria in 328, though his election was contested because he was too young for this position. He held his pastoral office for forty-six years, punctuated by five periods of exile due to the fluctuating popularity of the Nicene party. His seasons of exile proved providential, allowing him to cultivate relationships with like-minded leaders in the West and learn from ascetics in the Egyptian desert. The latter experience put him in contact with the famous Antony, and Athanasius later wrote his biography, *The Life of Antony*. Over time, the theology of Athanasius, Didymus the Blind, Basil of Caesarea, Gregory of Nyssa, and Gregory of Nazianzus became touchpoints of Nicene orthodoxy.

On the Incarnation provides Athanasius's pastoral argument for the necessity of Christ's incarnation: adding full humanity to his full divinity. Athanasius called this explanation of the incarnation and its centrality to the Christian faith "an elementary instruction and an outline of the faith in Christ and his divine manifestation to us."[1] The incarnation of Christ is fundamental to gospel belief, and nothing is more vital and transformative than that God was made flesh. The eternal Word made flesh, through whom God created all things and in whom all things hold together, is the center of our faith (John 1:1–3). Christ's work of salvation had to occur through the incarnation, for our decaying humanity needed redemption through both his humanity *and* divinity.[2] David Gwynn notes, "For Athanasius . . . the full significance of the Incarnation lay in bridging the gulf that separated God and creation and enabling humanity to 'become divine.'"[3] (In chapter 6, we consider how humanity "become[s] divine" by exploring transformation and sanctification.)

Our salvation by Christ's incarnation is not merely pragmatic; instead, it reshapes the vision of our life in the flesh and our future life in glory. Having received the redemption of our souls, we will also see the redemption of our bodies in eternity. Christ in his full humanity and divinity is the only one capable of accomplishing this feat. Jesus died knowing the greater good he achieved by being the true life himself. Athanasius explains: "So something wonderful and marvelous happened: that ignominious death which they thought to inflict, this was the trophy of his victory over death."[4] The ignominy of the crucifixion, indeed the worst form of death

---

[1] *On the Incarnation* 56.

[2] For a helpful summary of Athanasius's logic of salvation based on Christ's incarnation, see Alister McGrath, *Historical Theology: An Introduction to the History of Christian Thought,* 2nd ed. (Wiley-Blackwell, 2013), 43–46.

[3] David M. Gwynn, *Athanasius of Alexandria: Bishop, Theologian, Ascetic, Father*, Christian Theology in Context (Oxford University Press, 2012), 66.

[4] *On the Incarnation* 24.

conjured by man, was entirely overturned and reconstituted. Once a seat of shame, the cross is now a symbol of victory. Once only torture for the subjugated, the cross is now the token of the liberated. It defines salvation and fuels discipleship. As the writer of Hebrews instructs, "Let us run with endurance the race that lies before us, keeping our eyes on Jesus, the pioneer and perfecter of our faith. For the joy that lay before him, he endured the cross, despising the shame, and sat down at the right hand of the throne of God" (Heb 12:1b–2). In similar words, Athanasius asserts, "For we were the purpose of his embodiment, and for our salvation he so loved human beings as to come to be and appear in a human body."[5]

The creed contends, and Athanasius affirms, that salvation requires Christ's full humanity and full divinity. Though the language of this two-nature Christology was not fully articulated until the Council of Chalcedon in 451, we ought to consider this mystery is necessary for our salvation. As the creed affirms, Christ "descended . . . and became incarnate . . . for us humans and for our salvation." Let that sink in: "for us humans and for our salvation." Salvation begins with the incarnation. Evangelicals typically equate salvation with atonement, which is undoubtedly a significant and crucial element, but redemption includes salvation *and* a transformed life. Often, our Reformation reflexes fire at the notion of including our own works and virtuous acts in salvation. If we say that our works add to the salvation of God, then we are in trouble. Yet, early Christian thinkers found it impossible to talk about a salvation lacking the fruit of salvation also present in the believer's life. What we distinguish as a doctrine of sanctification, the early church rolled into the entire conversation about salvation. This explains what Athanasius says near

[5] *On the Incarnation* 4.

the end of *On the Incarnation*: "But in addition to the study and true knowledge of the scriptures, there is needed a good life and a pure soul and the virtue which is according to Christ, so that the mind, guided by it, may be able to attain and comprehend what it desires, as far as it is possible for human nature to learn about the God Word."[6] The beauty of salvation is based on the object of our faith and the fruit of our faith.

Athanasius reflected on the glorious nature of our salvation through the Son in his work *Against the Arians*. This work, composed of four discourses, sought to dismantle Arians and Arian-like ideas. According to Athanasius, the Arians are to be scorned as "neither having studied Scripture, nor understanding Christianity at all, and the faith which it contains." He understood that the scriptural language required an interpretation based on the *regula fidei,* or rule of faith.[7] This rule, used by Christians from the earliest generations, simply affirms the Trinity and the biblical story of redemption. By recognizing the basic biblical narrative of God, Christ, the Spirit, and salvation, we can better interpret individual Scripture passages within this scope. Consider two critical biblical texts in Athanasius's discourse and learn how he maintains an orthodox framework. The first important text Athanasius interprets is Prov 8:22–23: "The Lord created me as the beginning of his ways for his works; before the current age, in the beginning, before he made the world, he established me."[8] The Septuagint rendering in English is necessary to grasp the weight of the issue. While modern English translations avoid this issue by using the Masoretic (Hebrew) text, the fourth-century Fathers wrestled over these words as read in the Greek Old

---

[6] *On the Incarnation* 57.

[7] See Everett Ferguson, *The Rule of Faith: A Guide*, Cascade Companions 20 (Wipf and Stock, 2015).

[8] Prov 8:22–23 LXX (translation by Coleman M. Ford).

Testament. The Greek verb κτίζω (*ktizō*; "to create") did not bother Athanasius. He was careful to maintain that the personification of Wisdom in Proverbs was not equivalent to Christ being called the "wisdom of God" (1 Cor 1:24). Athanasius contended that "this mere term 'He created' does not necessarily signify the essence or the generation but indicates something else as coming to pass in Him of whom it speaks, and not simply that He who is said to be created, is at once in His Nature and Essence a creature."[9] Solomon recognized, in some incipient way, the Wisdom of God, which was finally revealed in Christ; he certainly did not make an ontological statement.[10] Athanasius affirms that Christ "says not, 'Before the world He founded me as Word or Son,' but simply, 'He founded me,' to show again, as I have said, that not for His own sake but for those who are built upon Him does He here also speak, after the way of proverbs."[11] The terms "created," "formed," and "founded" correspond to language used to describe eternal generation and the incarnation, both of which are distinct from God's creative activity of the world. We can look to Proverbs and other Old Testament texts, Athanasius believed, to find ways of talking about Christ, but we should never make illegitimate assertions about his nature.[12]

---

[9] *c. Ar.*, 2.19, 45.

[10] For more on Athanasius's reading of Prov 8 in *de Decretis* (i.e., Athanasius's defense of the creed), see Amy Brown Hughes and Shawn J. Wilhite, "The Beginnings of a Pro-Nicene Trinitarian Vision: Athanasius of Alexandria on the Activity of the Son and the Spirit," in *On Classical Trinitarianism: Retrieving the Nicene Doctrine of the Triune God*, ed. Matthew Barrett (IVP Academic, 2024).

[11] *c. Ar.*, 2.22, 74.

[12] For more on this idea as it relates to Prov 8, Athanasius, and Partitive exegesis, see Shawn J. Wilhite, *Cyril of Alexandria's Christological Exegesis: Explorations of Partitive Exegesis in the Dialogues on the Trinity*, Studia Traditionis Theologiae 70 (Brepols, 2026).

Next, Athanasius considered Phil 2:9–10: "For this reason God highly exalted him and gave him the name that is above every name, so that at the name of Jesus every knee will bow—in heaven and on earth and under the earth." On the surface of this text, Arians may seem to have a point. The Son appears to be subordinate to the Father, and though Jesus will be the object of devotion "in heaven and on earth and under the earth," the Father is still at the top, and Christ is his created agent. Thus, the Father gave the Son an exalted name, so the Arians argue, as a grace. Athanasius, on the other hand, had none of that: "For if He was not, or was indeed, but afterwards was promoted, how were all things made by Him, or how in Him, were He not perfect, did the Father delight?"[13] Athanasius identified here a major interpretive issue with Arius's thought. Perfection requires full divinity, and the acts attributed to Christ are impossible if he did not possess a perfect and unalterable divinity in his nature.

Thus, the truth of the Son's divinity is the opposite of what Arius claimed. Athanasius makes the case:

> Therefore, if, even before the world was made, the Son had that glory, and was Lord of glory and the Highest, and descended from heaven, and is ever to be worshipped, it follows that He had not promotion from His descent, but rather Himself promoted the things which needed promotion; and if He descended to effect their promotion, therefore He did not receive in reward the name of the Son and God, but rather He Himself has made us sons of the Father, and defied men by becoming Himself man.[14]

Athanasius read the text with the priority of Christ's full divinity and humanity in mind. This is not "eisegesis" but a theological

---

[13] *c. Ar.*, 1.11, 38.

[14] *c. Ar.*, 1.11, 38.

reading that corresponds to the economy of God's salvation while actively engaging with the text of Scripture. We ought to bring basic orthodox presuppositions to the text to read it correctly. This does not bend the text to an external agenda but confirms and makes sense of what the text already declares: The eternal Son is Christ the Lord.

Becoming Divine

The incarnation, for Athanasius, has the effect of *divinizing humanity*—yes, you read that correctly. A necessary component of salvation is that humankind is divinized. Athanasius declared, "For he was incarnate that we might be made god."[15] The doctrine that has come to be called *theosis*, or *deification*, derives from this related idea of the Fathers.[16] While this manner of speaking about salvation does not seem typical to Protestants, the basic notion pertains much more to our doctrine of sanctification.

Because of Christ's work on our behalf, we are more than saved from punishment (as amazing as that is); we are now mysteriously dwelling in the life of God. As we have mentioned in chapter 4, we believe this is what the apostle Peter was aiming at when he said, "His divine power has given us everything required for life and godliness through the knowledge of him who called us by his own glory and goodness" (2 Pet 1:3). Peter highlights all the ways Christians

---

[15] *On the Incarnation* 54.

[16] For a summary of deification see C. M. Ford, "Deification," ed. Michael A. G. Haykin, *The Essential Lexham Dictionary of Church History* (Lexham, 2022). For a good one-volume work on deification in Greek patristic thought, see Norman Russell, *The Doctrine of Deification in the Greek Patristic Tradition* (Oxford University Press, 2004). For an assessment of deification in Latin Christianity see Jared Ortiz, ed. *Deification in the Latin Patristic Tradition* (Catholic University of America Press, 2019).

ought to grow in holiness and virtue by nature of being in the life of God through Christ. Whatever might be meant by *theosis* in Athanasius's thought, the mystery of sharing in the divine nature is best captured in our understanding of *sanctification*. We grow in holiness and virtue because of God's work of bringing us into his life through Jesus Christ. We indeed are made *godlike*, divinized, not equal to God as he is in his nature, but connected to his life through Christ. Athanasius also aligns with this understanding: "[Christ] manifested himself through a body that we might receive an idea of the invisible Father; and he endured the insults of human beings, that we might inherit incorruptibility."[17]

Gregory of Nazianzus on the Beauty of Salvation

Gregory of Nazianzus (c. 329–390) possessed a well-educated, academic mind and studied in Athens, where he met Basil of Caesarea. Along with his studies, he desired monastic spiritual reflection, though his father prompted him to instead pursue pastoral ministry. Having finally accepted the pastoral call, he famously left the pastoral office, only to reluctantly return. He took his subsequent ministry post at the request of his friend Basil and became the bishop of the small provincial town of Sasima (near modern-day Hasanköy, Turkey) before eventually taking on Constantinople's bishopric for a short time.

We consider Gregory's orations because they provide a thoroughly biblical, profoundly logical, and refreshingly spiritual reflection on God, salvation, and the hope of humanity. When reading Gregory's sermons, one must consider the Eunomian heresy coloring the background: Eunomians were generally sympathetic to

---

[17] *On the Incarnation* §54.

"Arian" ideas, eventually rejecting the full divinity of Christ.[18] In the first of these five orations (*Oration* 27), Gregory addressed those who "have undermined every approach to true religion by their complete obsession with setting and solving conundrums."[19] Gregory addresses the problematic overindulgence in speculation that suppresses the mystery of God. While we can know God through his Word and work, the Eunomians and others divided the godhead, thereby overlooking his glory. Gregory asserts that our knowledge on this side of eternity is incomplete, though we ought to grow through Spirit-led biblical exploration. In his *Oration* 28, the second of the five, Gregory assesses the doctrine of God, while noting his own "frailty" in undertaking such a task. Remarking on the beauty and order of creation, Gregory draws a helpful comparison: "No one seeing a beautifully elaborated lyre with its harmonious, orderly arrangement, and hearing the lyre's music will fail to form a notion of its craftsman-player, to recur to him in thought though ignorant of him by sight. In this way the creative power, which moves and safeguards its objects, is clear to us, though it be not grasped by the understanding."[20]

---

[18] Eunomius was an *anomoian* ("not of same substance") teacher in Cappadocia, consistently asserting the Son was not of the same nature as the Father. Both Basil and then his brother Gregory of Nyssa wrote against his teaching. A defrocked bishop, he led several people to form a schismatic community until his death in 394. For a summary of the controversy, see the Saint Basil of Caesarea, *Against Eunomius*, trans. Mark DelCogliano and Andrew Radde-Gallwitz, Fathers of the Church (Catholic University of America Press, 2011), 3–55.

[19] *Oration* 27.2 in St Gregory of Nazianzus, *On God and Christ: The Five Theological Orations and Two Letters to Cledonius*, ed. John Behr, trans. Frederick Williams and Lionel Wickham, Popular Patristics Series (St Vladimir's Seminary Press, 2002), 25.

[20] *Oration* 28.6.

Clearly, "dissolution is utterly alien to God the prime nature . . . [and] no dissolution means no division; no division means no conflict; no conflict means no composition, and hence no body involving composition."[21]

The otherworldly cosmic redemption guaranteed by Christ's life, death, and resurrection makes salvation beautiful in the Christian perspective. The Incorruptible One secured what we corrupted ones could not. In Christ, God's created image bearers move away from disintegration and back toward oneness with God.

No "Because" Required

Later in his *Oration* 28, Gregory describes the task of theology in terms of a massive building project using the smallest of tools. Inviting his hearers to consider the entirety of creation, Gregory explains the intricacies of animal and plant life. Why do this? Gregory addresses our finite nature and challenges our ability to comprehend even the basics of the created order, not to mention the mysterious nature of God and redemption. If we have trouble wrapping our minds around biology, how can we even begin to comprehend the grand schemes of the Creator? God's salvation cannot be fathomed with the mind and senses alone; it must be received by faith in the deep recesses of our hearts. When confronted with the majesty and mystery of God, all we can do is either accept it with humility or reject it with utter pride. While wondering at the immensity of the sea, consider the awe of God who created it and set all things in motion, including the work of salvation in Christ. Gregory ended his sermon pondering: "[I have] been engaged in a struggle to prove that even the nature of beings on the

---

[21] *Oration* 28.7.

second level is too much for our minds, let alone God's primal and unique, not to say all-transcending nature."[22]

While *Oration* 28 does not directly mention the work of salvation, its implications are clear: finite man cannot comprehend the plans of God. In Orations 29 and 30, Gregory argues for the necessity of Christ and the work of the Son in accomplishing redemption. After discussing the eternal generation of the Son, Gregory implores his hearers to consider the biblical reality of Christ's divinity and humanity, mainly referencing New Testament passages. What seems to be a series of contradictions, or textual ammunition for heretics, are, in fact, necessary descriptions to articulate the beautiful union of Christ's humanity with his divinity. Both exist in exquisite harmony, for: "[he] remained what he was; what he was not, he assumed. No 'because' is required for his existence in the beginning, for what could account for the existence of God."[23] If Gregory could have typed the flexed bicep emoji (💪), we are sure he would have included one after this statement.

Biblical Connections

As with nearly every early church father, both Athanasius and Gregory argued their position using close reading of Scripture, with an open Bible in hand. In light of this example, we marvel at the rich spiritual truth contained in John 1:1–14. "In the beginning," as John witnesses in John 1:1, "was the Word, and the Word was with God, and the Word was God." John makes both a biblical assertion and a philosophical connection. The Word is eternal (i.e., before the beginning), is God (as whatever God is by nature, so is

[22] *Oration* 28.9.

[23] *Oration* 29.19.

the Word), and with God (united with God the Father and Spirit). The Word, or *Logos*, is the operating agent of all wisdom and reality. The Word is simultaneously an instrument of the Father and himself God; though an instrument, we should never assume the Son is less in divinity and glory. In becoming human, the Word made flesh became the light for creation (John 1:5, 9).

Commentator Colin Kruse observes, "To *receive* him means, as this verse indicates, to believe in his name. To believe in a person's name is to believe in the person, because the name stands for the person. Receiving him involves accepting the teaching and revelation of God (the 'light') he brought."[24] To believe in Christ is to place one's complete trust and allegiance in God's light! This only makes sense if he is worthy of such confidence. Christ, being both God and man, truly deserves our fidelity and loving obedience. The truth that the eternal Son took on flesh for our salvation is core to the gospel proclamation. The Fathers at Nicaea understood this, and thus, to mitigate or jettison this conviction leads to a compromise in the gospel message. D. A. Carson adds: "This is the supreme revelation. If we are to know God, neither rationalism nor irrational mysticism will suffice: the former reduces God to mere object, and the latter abandons all controls."[25] Special revelation in the form of Christ's incarnation is the content of our salvation. Only a humble and Spirit-wrought acceptance of Christ as the incarnate Lord constitutes saving faith.

John's opening declaration of Christ's incarnation also points to the glory of the Son. John and others were witnesses to the glory of

---

[24] Colin G. Kruse, *John: An Introduction and Commentary*, ed. Eckhard J. Schnabel, 2nd ed., vol. 4, Tyndale New Testament Commentaries (IVP Academic, 2017), 61, emphasis original.

[25] D. A. Carson, *The Gospel According to John*, The Pillar New Testament Commentary (Eerdmans, 1991), 127.

Christ. Beauty is a less-recognized synonym for glory. The apostles looked on the cosmic beauty of God in the incarnation, including in the death, burial, resurrection, and ascension of Jesus Christ. This glory, or beauty, "the glory of the one and only Son from the Father," is not a mere grace given to the Son as a divine creature, as Arian thought describes. God's glory cannot be replicated, for he declares, "I am the LORD; that is my name; my glory I give to no other" (Isa 42:8 ESV). Pure beauty from the divine nature is fully present in and manifested by the Son, and in whom we are now united. Our salvation is possible only through the glorious Son. We echo what Carson notes: "The glory displayed in the incarnate Word is the kind of glory a father grants to his one and only, best-loved Son—and this 'father' is God himself. Thus, it is nothing less than God's glory that John and his friends witnessed in the Word-made-flesh."[26] John and the New Testament resound with this simple yet life-altering truth: no incarnation, no salvation.

Conclusion

While trying to capture the wondrous beauty of the incarnation and its effects, Athanasius expressed, "Therefore it is better not to seek to speak of the whole, of which one cannot even speak of a part, but rather to recall one thing, and leave the whole for you to marvel at. For all are equally marvelous, and wherever one looks, seeing there the divinity of the Word, one is struck with exceeding awe."[27] Like one who gazes "at the expanse of the sea" and attempts to count the waves, Christians cannot even begin to "comprehend the achievements of Christ in the body."[28] The problem with the Arian and

---

[26] Carson, *The Gospel According to John*, 128.

[27] *On the Incarnation* 54.

[28] *On the Incarnation* 54.

Eunomian vision of God, according to Athanasius and Gregory, is its narrowness. When we purge the mystery of God, we are left with a God unworthy of worship. The beauty and majesty of salvation through Christ fuels our worship and permits us to revel in God's extraordinary but inexplicable love and mercy. Nicaea and its pro-Nicene defenders wished to ensure that Christians maintained this proper view of salvation so that they would gaze at the splendor of the triune God and be transformed as a result.

CHAPTER 6

"The Trophy over Death": The Beauty of Spiritual Transformation

[We believe] in the Holy Spirit, the Lord and giver of life, who proceeds from the Father [and the Son], who is worshipped and glorified together with the Father and the Son, [and] who has spoken through the prophets.

—The Niceno-Constantinople Creed (381)

Now the Lord is the Spirit, and where the Spirit of the Lord is, there is freedom. And we all, with unveiled face, beholding the glory of the Lord, are being transformed into the same image from one degree of glory to another. For this comes from the Lord who is the Spirit.

—2 Corinthians 3:17–18 (ESV)

Thinking Nicenely Today: The death and resurrection of Christ is an eternally significant moment in time and space. It defines the course of every person united to Christ by faith who willingly gives his or her allegiance to him and begins the ongoing transformation by the power of the Holy Spirit as we await Christ's glorious return. The Spirit is the giver of life through the Son, joining us to God's life.

In the previous chapter, we introduced the idea of trophies, relaying Christ's victory over sin and death as the ultimate trophy envisioned by Athanasius. This talk of trophies reminds me (Coleman) of the first time the Dallas Mavericks, my hometown NBA team, won the league championship in 2011. At the time, I was leading a few dozen teenagers at a church camp in Orange Beach, Alabama. We kept up with the final games of the series between the Mavericks and the Miami Heat, and when Dallas won the championship, we were in a hot and smelly church bus! If you know me, you know I am not a huge sports fan, but this was a momentous win for anyone from North Texas. Seeing Dirk Nowitzki, Jason "the Jet" Terry, Shawn Marion, Jason Kidd, and Tyson Chandler embrace one another to celebrate was beyond description. The team lifted the championship trophy in the air, and all the fans of the once beleaguered, underdog Dallas team experienced the victory together. It was as if every fan was in Miami with the team, tasting the glory of the championship win. True, it was the players who had done the work of consistent practice; performed countless hours of drills; provided the strength, skill, and agility to the game; and fought tirelessly to beat the Miami Heat. Yet, it felt like a victory for every Dallas fan. Their trophy was our trophy.

In a much more eternally significant way, Christ's life, death, burial, and resurrection become ours through the life-giving Spirit. Christ was the perfect sacrifice and ransom for humanity. When the Word took on flesh and appeared among us, reality as we know it was forever transformed. We who are in Christ receive all the benefits of his work, including the Holy Spirit, who brings about ongoing transformation. In chapter 5, we explored how the death of Jesus—the Word who took on flesh—was a glorious and universe-shattering moment in time. Salvation began at the incarnation, was secured at the cross, was magnified at the resurrection, and will be completed at his return. The event of salvation, from crucifixion to resurrection and glorification, is the trophy of Christians who pledge their allegiance to Christ and the vital object of our ongoing transformation. Paul contends, "In him you also were sealed with the promised Holy Spirit when you heard the word of truth, the gospel of your salvation, and when you believed. The Holy Spirit is the down payment of our inheritance, until the redemption of the possession, to the praise of his glory" (Eph 1:13–14). While Nicaea does not define every detail of Christ's work of salvation or the work of the Spirit, the hope and biblical structure of salvation is provided in the creed. Athanasius declared, "Death having been put to death by him, what else should happen than that the body should rise and be shown as the trophy over it?"[1]

In his very person, Jesus Christ became what Athanasius called "the trophy of death," for all time and for all people who are united to him by faith and pledge allegiance to him as Lord. In this chapter, we build on the discussion in chapter 5 on the wonder and beauty of salvation and hint at the work of the Spirit (knowing there is still more to discover). We explore the magnitude and manifest beauty of Christ's work for us. We confess again that the death and resurrection of the Word made flesh secures for us what no other could: complete salvation. In this

---

[1] *On the Incarnation*, 30.

chapter, we build on this idea as it extends to our sanctification, our ongoing transformation by the Spirit in Christ, of which our "trophy of death" is the genesis and ongoing focus. The notion of sanctification, or growing in holiness, is rooted in Christ's finished work and the Spirit's beginning work. Hence, any discussion of salvation must include its application to daily life. To help us understand the nature of spiritual transformation, we look again at Athanasius's thought as he meditated on Scripture and the work of Christ.

Understanding the Victory of Christ

Admittedly, the victory motif of Christ's atonement (also known as *Christus Victor*) has not been as prevalent among evangelicals. Still, it has warrant among Protestants such as Martin Luther and John Calvin.[2] Protestants generally focus more on atonement for sin in the death of Christ than the theme of victory over death, but this need not be the case.[3] Christ's death was one of victory for our salvation.

This victory theme in Christ's life, death, and resurrection informed Athanasius's rhetoric and gave him the theological purpose he needed to consistently refute the machinations of Arian theology. If Christ is just a being, albeit the highest of the created beings, then his death and resurrection could not have accomplished everything the Scriptures claim it has. Christ's victory

---

[2] Robert Kolb, "Christus Victor," *TGC Concise Theology*, https://www.thegospelcoalition.org/essay/christus-victor/.

[3] For the classic single-volume treatment of *Christus Victor* in Christian thought, see Gustaf Aulén, *Christus Victor: An Historical Study of the Three Main Types of the Idea of Atonement*, trans. A. G. Hebert (Wipf and Stock, 2003).

over death itself cannot be final if Christ is a mere creature. One scholar notes, "The distinctive trait of Athanasius's representation of God is its strong soteriological emphasis, which prevails to such a degree as to profoundly influence the christological and trinitarian discourse."[4] The saving incarnation of Christ radically informs how we talk about Christ and even God himself as the Trinity. Christ's glorified body gives us a new pattern for humanity and a model for this life as we imitate Christ's thoughts and actions (see 1 John 2:5–6).

The life of Christ is worthy of imitation and is the standard for all Christian virtue. This is no mere "What Would Jesus Do?" Christianity but a sound pattern for us to follow, as people empowered by the Spirit in a community of other Christ-followers. This new pattern of humanity also models our life to come in eternity. Paul declares this beautiful truth to the church: "When this corruptible body is clothed with incorruptibility, and this mortal body is clothed with immortality, then the saying that is written will take place: Death has been swallowed up in victory. Where, death, is your victory? Where, death, is your sting?" (1 Cor 15:54–55). By understanding the future state of our glorified, bodily perfection with Christ, we gain a greater perspective of our current circumstances, leading to greater hope and perseverance in this life. Christ's victory is manifold in its power, potential, and purposes. This motif propelled Athanasius to consistently argue for the biblical truth of Christ's full divinity and humanity and its transforming effects.

---

[4] Alberto Camplani, "Athanasius of Alexandria," ed. Angelo Di Berardino and James Hoover, trans. Joseph T. Papa, Erik A. Koenke, and Eric E. Hewett, *Encyclopedia of Ancient Christianity* (IVP Academic, 2014), 1:281.

Athanasius on Christ's Victory over Death

Athanasius was a fervent voice for Nicene orthodoxy, but he, like many church fathers, was not a controversialist for controversy's sake. At times, his rhetoric was bullish, but his times demanded such ferocity. In his analysis, Christopher Stead does not find Athanasius's rhetoric appropriate for our times, though Khaled Anatolios gives a much more positive assessment.[5] Most of the fathers were active pastors leading their local churches by preaching, teaching, and practicing a soul-care ministry.[6] In his direct confrontation of Arius's theology, Athanasius produces some of the most theologically rich and biblically saturated tomes of church history. In *On the Incarnation*, Athanasius minces no words about the person and work of Christ: "[A]t the very trophy over death, I mean the cross, all creation confessed that he who was made known and suffered in the body was not simply a human being but Son of God and Savior of all."[7] This idea of "trophy over death" is a consistent image and theme in Athanasius's thought.

Greek Orthodox scholar Philip Kariatlis observes:

> [Athanasius's] salvific vision is presented here with much clarity, coherence, and comprehensiveness: salvation was not achieved merely through the conception and birth of the Son of God by Mary, but included Christ's entire life, namely his 'divine manifestation' culminating with

---

[5] G. Christopher Stead. "Rhetorical Method in Athanasius." *Vigiliae Christianae* 30, no. 2 (June 1976): 121–37; Khaled Anatolios, "'When was God without wisdom?': Trinitarian hermeneutics and rhetorical strategy in Athanasius," *Studia Patristica* 41 (2006): 117–23.

[6] See Coleman M. Ford and Shawn J. Wilhite, *Ancient Wisdom for the Care of Souls: Learning the Art of Ministry from the Church Fathers* (Crossway, 2024).

[7] *On the Incarnation,* 19.

> the cross and resurrection. St Athanasius incorporates the entire life and work of Christ into his soteriological plan thus presenting it in its widest scope. The incarnation initiated the process of salvation by bestowing upon humanity a growing 'piety' of Jesus Christ.[8]

Christ's death has a multiplicity of meanings and applications for humanity, particularly those who are in the life of God through faith in Christ. Athanasius's portrayal of Christ is more than just a discussion of divine biology. The incarnation is a full-throated cry of freedom from death and of transformation of the human experience.

According to Athanasius, Christ takes what is shameful in the world and completely subverts it in the divine economy. No one in the first century would have thought a cross could be an object of liberation; it was a cruel reminder of imperial subjugation, a threat to would-be naysayers that someone more powerful was in charge. But God delights, as Paul tells us, to take "what is foolish in the world to shame the wise" and take what is "weak in the world to shame the strong" (1 Cor 1:27). Thus, Athanasius declared, "So something wonderful and marvelous happened: that ignominious death which they thought to inflict, this was the trophy of his victory over death."[9]

In Ancient Rome, when army generals were victorious in battle, especially those that dramatically increased the wealth and prestige of Rome, the senate might grant them a "triumph." This was an official ceremony and military parade, to display the spoils and trophies of war. An example of a triumph can be seen on the Arch of Titus, still on display in Rome today, which depicts the general

[8] Philip Kariatlis, "Soteriological Insights in St Athanasius' On the Incarnation, *Phronema* 28, no. 2 (2013): 27–28.

[9] *On the Incarnation* 24.

Titus (soon to be emperor) in his triumph parade, which was held to commemorate his sack of Jerusalem in AD 71. The wares of the Jewish temple, including a giant menorah, are seen being carried by Roman troops.

These were the trophies—the riches—of Titus's victory. Now imagine if those priceless objects were replaced with a depiction of a bloody wooden cross. Nothing would have been more repugnant to a first-century person. It would have made no sense to them to see a cross depicted as a trophy of victory. Yet, this is how Athanasius depicts the triumph of Christ: Jesus's march through the streets of Jerusalem to Golgotha was his victory march, as he displayed the trophy he used to slay humanity's most significant enemy: death. Christ is the victorious warrior who conquers death!

Gregory of Nazianzus reflected on the tension of the Word taking on flesh for our sake and our salvation:

> He who is comes into being, and the uncreated is created, and the uncontained is contained, through the intervention of the rational soul, which mediates between the divinity and the coarseness of flesh. The one who makes rich becomes poor; he is made poor in my flesh, that I might be enriched through his divinity. The full one empties himself; for he empties himself of his own glory for a short time, that I may participate in his fullness. What is the wealth of his goodness? What is this mystery concerning me? I participated in the [divine] image, and I did not keep it; he participates in my flesh both to save the image and to make the flesh immortal.[10]

---

[10] *Oration* 41.9 in Nonna Verna Harrison, trans., *St Gregory of Nazianzus: Festal Orations*, Popular Patristics Series 36 (St Vladimir's Seminary Press, 2008), 169.

Fig. 6.1. Arch of Titus. Image from Wikipedia Commons (https://commons.wikimedia.org/wiki/File:Arch_of_Titus_(Roma).jpg)

Fig. 6.2. Relief showing the sack of Jerusalem. Image from Axel Smid, Unsplash (https://unsplash.com/photos/a-close-up-of-a-building-with-a-tree-in-the-background-egg6rxoWt0c)

Human language and concepts are incapable of capturing divine mystery. As Gregory related, we are "enriched through his divinity" so that we "may participate in his fullness."[11] This enriching and participatory process describes the essence of our transformation. Divine participation is another way to describe the doctrine and process of deification, or *theosis*, discussed in chapter 5. Reflecting on this relationship of participation in Latin and Eastern Christian traditions, Norman Russell states, "Theosis is thus an ascent to the vision of God, which is the vision of truth, yet it is not the result of a purely intellectual process. It is participation in a divine power . . . that calls for intuitive apprehension . . . [and] requires the presence of faith."[12] As envisioned by pro-Nicene theologians, this process must include the Spirit, who is divine in the same manner as the Son and Father. Writing to Serapion, an Egyptian bishop from AD 339 to c. 359, Athanasius exclaimed, "Who will join you to God if you do not have the Spirit of God himself but the spirit of the created order?"[13] As scholars note, "this new context [of pro-Nicene trinitarianism] led to a recovery of pneumatology which emphasized the Spirit's status as Creator within the inseparable and unmediated creative activity of God."[14] Without the Spirit as Lord and giver of life, there is no true transformation.

---

[11] *Oration* 38.13 (Harrison, 70).

[12] Norman Russell, *Theosis and Religion: Participation in Divine Life in the Eastern and Western Traditions*, Cambridge Studies in Religion, Philosophy, and Society (Cambridge University Press, 2024), 97.

[13] *Letter* 1.29.2 in Mark DelCogliano, Andrew Radde-Gallwitz, and Lewis Ayres, trans., *Works on the Spirit: Athanasius's Letters to Serapion on the Holy Spirit, and, Didymus's on the Holy Spirit*, Popular Patristics Series 43 (St Vladimir's Seminary Press, 2011), 98.

[14] DelCogliano, Radde-Gallwitz, and Ayres, "General Introduction," in *Works on the Spirit*, 14.

This process of sanctification is beautifully depicted in Gregory of Nyssa's *Life of Moses*. One line in particular strikes us: "[W]e regard falling from God's friendship as the only thing dreadful and we consider becoming God's friend the only thing worthy of honor and desire. This, as I have said, is the perfection of life."[15] Brian Daley observes, "In Gregory's theology, mutability is one of the defining aspects of created being: creatures are always *becoming*, always growing to be either more or less of what they are made to be. . . . As a result, the perfection of creatures is *always a process of growth in this participation*—a growth that never comes to an end, precisely because the finite can never completely possess the infinite."[16] More than an antiquated philosophical concept, participation compelled Athanasius, Gregory of Nyssa, and other pro-Nicene fathers. We grow in friendship with God by participating in his life through the incarnation and resurrection of Christ by the Spirit. By faith, those who have received the salvation God offers in Christ come to live in his divine life as friends. God initiates and sustains our transformation, and we cohere with God through our active growth in Christlike virtue. The Spirit, the Lord and giver of life, perpetuates this growth as we actively obey and follow Christ.

Christ's additional trophy is his incorruptible and impassible resurrected body. This body testifies to all creation that death was no longer master over it. The period between his final breath on the cross and his first breath as a resurrected and glorified human showed the world that his death was genuine. Nothing was staged,

---

[15] *Life of Moses* 2.320 in Abraham J. Malherbe and Everett Ferguson, trans., *Gregory of Nyssa: The Life of Moses*, The Classics of Western Spirituality (Paulist Press, 1978), 137.

[16] Brian E. Daley, *God Visible: Patristic Christology Reconsidered* (Oxford University Press, 2018), 140 (emphasis ours).

nothing was doctored, and it was an actual death. Christ alone can carry the trophies of the cross and his body through the cosmic triumph of eternity. Athanasius asserts, "Now, if it is by the sign of the cross and by the faith that is in Christ that death is trampled down, then, if judging by truth, it is none other than Christ himself who shows the trophies and victories against death and renders it fully weakened."[17]

How a Trophy Leads to Transformation

A Roman triumph honored and lauded the victorious general, giving him bragging rights for countless dinner parties. His victory, however, lived in the people's memory as a memory in the pages of Roman history. His triumph was never intended to radically shape the character of any other person. This is not the case with the triumph of Christ. His victory is a ripple in the fabric of space and time. The victory of Christ was not a footnote in history; it changed the trajectory of history entirely. To look to Christ's victory in faith is to be transformed forever. Athanasius beautifully unpacks the transforming effects of Christ's victory using the imagery of darkness and light:

> For as, if after the night the sun appears and every earthly place is enlightened by it, there is no doubt at all that the sun, spreading its light out everywhere, is also the one chasing away the darkness and illuminating everything, so also, with death being despised and trampled down since the saving manifestation of the Savior in the body and the conclusion of the cross, it is clear that he is the Savior,

[17] *On the Incarnation* 29.

> being revealed in the body, destroying death, and daily displaying the trophies against it in his disciples.[18]

This daily, ongoing display of light that comes from his victory shows how the church transforms and grows in holiness through their identification with the victorious Savior. The disciples of Christ are to reflect Christ's victory, "daily displaying the trophies against [death]" in themselves.[19]

In light of our identification with Christ, consider the nature of idolatry and its effects on the human heart. There is no neutral idol; anything we give our heart to must, by necessity, conform our heart to its desires and will. If idols are demonic, then they necessarily conform the heart to evil, even if that evil is not readily apparent in one's life. Athanasius observes that the work of Christ transforms many who once followed the way of idols. He asserts: "So all Gentiles from everywhere, rejecting the inherited customs and the godlessness of idols, place their hope henceforth in Christ and dedicate themselves to him, so that one can also see such things with the eyes themselves."[20] The cosmic victory of Christ applied by the power of the Holy Spirit is the only explanation for this phenomenon.

According to Athanasius, those who have pledged allegiance to Christ have a new ability to see clearly. They see their former life of sin and idolatry for what it is: madness and folly. Godlessness has been replaced with true godliness. By looking to Christ, those who once followed a path of destruction are transformed. Salvation brings dramatic change: a new way of seeing, a new way of living,

---

[18] *On the Incarnation* 29.

[19] *On the Incarnation* 29.

[20] *On the Incarnation* 37.

and a new way of being in the world. Transformation by the Spirit is always the fruit of salvation.

Other pro-Nicene fathers were somewhat united concerning the transformative effects of salvation. To cite one prominent example, in his *Regulae Moralia* or *Ethics*, Basil the Great, bishop of Caesarea (330–378) provided a thorough exposition of the Christian life. His main question is how to live out a life of repentance and faith in Christ. Faith and repentance, Basil concludes, are marked by tangible, *physical* signs that "exhibit from the heart all else that is proper to repentance."[21] A person who truly understands the state of their soul and the beautiful work of Christ on their behalf can do nothing but weep for their state. This humble posture is part of what it means to "bear fruit of repentance," as echoed by John the Baptist in Luke 3:8. Basil is clear that those who continue living as one "opposed to godly piety" cannot serve God.[22] After being cleansed through faith in Christ, a Christian is bound for good works according to the holiness of God. Basil minces no words: "[T]he evidence of love is keeping the commandments of Christ in endurance of his sufferings even unto death."[23] This transformation, wrought by the Spirit, ought to mark a Christian for the remainder of their life. If someone has true faith, his or her present life will drastically differ from the former way of living and the life of the unbelieving neighbor.

Indeed, to confess and live by Christ properly, one must also confess and live by the Spirit. Basil asserts elsewhere, "I testify to anyone who refuses the Spirit that his faith in the Father and the

[21] *Ethics* 1.3 in Jacob N. Van Sickle, trans., *St. Basil the Great: On Christian Ethics*, Popular Patristics Series 51 (St Vladimir's Seminary Press, 2014), 105.

[22] *Ethics* 2.1.

[23] *Ethics* 3.2.

Son, which he cannot have without the simultaneous presence of the Spirit, will become fruitless for him."[24] Anyone who wishes to honor and glorify God confesses his or her need for the Spirit. The one saved by Christ embarks on the journey of transformation in Christ by the power of the Spirit. This is not a sinless perfection but a marked and ongoing change in word, thought, and deed. It is a movement from love of self alone to love of God and others, even love of one's enemies for the sake of God. No explanation can account for true transformation except for the work of Christ sustained by the Holy Spirit.

Athanasius summarizes the cosmos-shattering reality of Christ's work and its effects:

> When did human beings begin to abandon the worship of idols, except since the true God Word of God came among human beings? Or when have the oracles amongst the Greeks and everywhere ceased and become empty, except since the Savior revealed himself upon earth? Or when did those who are called gods and heroes by the poets begin to be condemned as merely mortal humans, except since the Lord erected the trophy over death and preserved incorruptible the body which he took, raising it from the dead? Or when were the deceit and madness of the demons despised, except when the Power of God, the Word, the Master of all, even of these, condescended, because of the weakness of humans, to appear on earth? When did the craft and teachings of magic begin to be trampled underfoot, except when the divine manifestation of the Word

[24] *On the Holy Spirit* 11, 27 in Stephen Hildebrand, trans., *St Basil the Great: On the Holy Spirit*, Popular Patristics Series 42 (St Vladimir's Seminary Press, 2011), 58.

> took place among human beings? And when, in short, did the wisdom of the Greeks become foolish (see 1 Cor 1:18–24) except when the true Wisdom of God revealed itself upon earth?[25]

The power of such a transformation cannot be understated. No one before and no one since has accomplished what Christ has done in his work and person.

Biblical Connections

Scripture clearly teaches Christ's victory over sin and death, spiritual transformation through the Spirit, and the life-giving effects of faith in Christ. In 1 Corinthians 15, Paul declares, "Death has been swallowed up in victory. Where, death, is your victory? Where, death, is your sting? The sting of death is sin, and the power of sin is the law. But thanks be to God, who gives us the victory through our Lord Jesus Christ!" (1 Cor 15:54–57). This victory is a conscious and ongoing reality, bringing perpetual renewal within the life of the church. Paul encourages Christians to "be steadfast, immovable, always excelling in the Lord's work" (1 Cor 15:58). The resurrection of Christ is both a historical reality and a spiritual foundation with ongoing implications. If Christ is raised, we have hope. If Christ is victorious over death, we are freed from the fear of death and separation from God. If Christ's victory is our own, we can walk in freedom from sin. The transformation is not instantaneous, but, as Paul reminds us, we are to continually be steadfast, immovable, and excelling in the work of the Lord.

Elsewhere Paul states, "For we know that our old self was crucified with him so that the body ruled by sin might be rendered

---

[25] *On the Incarnation* 46.

powerless so that we may no longer be enslaved to sin, since a person who has died is freed from sin" (Rom 6:6–7). Paul assumes Christ's death has a direct impact on our spiritual life. If we have indeed been "crucified with Christ" in a spiritual sense (Gal 2:20), then we are guaranteed resurrection of our physical bodies based on the life and work of Christ. We have been freed to live a beautiful life unto God for his glory. F. F. Bruce states, "Death pays all debts, so those who have died with Christ have the slate wiped clean, and are ready to begin their new life with Christ freed from the entail of the past."[26]

Finally, the apostle Peter clarifies that the resurrection gives us the power to persevere as we long for glory. Through Christ, God "has given us new birth into a living hope through the resurrection of Jesus Christ from the dead and into an inheritance that is imperishable, undefiled, and unfading, kept in heaven for you" (1 Pet 1:3–4). This lofty claim is buttressed by the on-the-ground reality that we grow in Christlikeness. Peter puts it this way: "You rejoice in this, even though now for a short time, if necessary, you suffer grief in various trials so that the proven character of your faith—more valuable than gold which, though perishable, is refined by fire—may result in praise, glory, and honor at the revelation of Jesus Christ" (1 Pet 1:6–7). Our transformation, Peter reminds us, is dotted along the path with moments and seasons of suffering, not because God is fickle but because God is faithful. Tom Schreiner summarizes, "God brings sufferings into the lives of believers to purify their faith and to demonstrate its genuineness. The eschatological reward reveals that believers have been transformed by God's grace, inasmuch as they rejoice in God so much they are willing

---

[26] F. F. Bruce, *Romans: An Introduction and Commentary*, Tyndale New Testament Commentaries 6 (IVP, 1985), 143.

to undergo pain."[27] Our Savior's victory guides believers along through seasons of joy as well as seasons of suffering, producing increased faith, hope, and love in Christ.

Conclusion

Athanasius concluded his work in *On the Incarnation* by imploring his reader to reflect on the wonder and majesty of Christ. This wonder ought to transform us with Christlike virtue by the power of the Spirit. Knowledge of Scripture, according to Athanasius, must be paired with "the virtue which is according to Christ," and thereby, we will attain what our soul longs for.[28] Like any dedicated fan who "feels" the victory of their championship team, we Christians ought to see ourselves as present in Christ's victory over death. We are the primary beneficiaries of his incarnational life, which includes his beautiful death and glorious resurrection. More than any championship trophy, Christ is an eternal trophy over death that can never be tarnished or destroyed. This trophy does not collect dust on a bedroom shelf but instead orients us to a beautiful, flourishing life here on earth. God has given us the Spirit to ensure our growth and apply Christ's work to our transformation. Our earthly trophies will surely fade and crumble, but God's eternal trophy over death will stand forever in glory.

---

[27] Thomas R. Schreiner, *1, 2 Peter, Jude*, The New American Commentary 37 (B&H, 2003), 68.

[28] *On the Incarnation* 57.

CHAPTER 7

"We Believe": The Beauty of Nicene Practices

[We believe] in one, holy, catholic, and apostolic church.
We confess one baptism for the forgiveness of sins.
—The Niceno-Constantinople Creed (381)

There is one body and one Spirit—just as you were called to the one hope that belongs to your call—one Lord, one faith, one baptism, one God and Father of all, who is over all and through all and in all.
—Ephesians 4:4–6 (ESV)

Thinking Nicenely Today: The church must thoughtfully use the Nicene Creed throughout the life of the church, including catechesis, in preparation for Baptism leading to the Eucharist (Lord's Supper), crafting theological statements of faith, preparation for preaching, and training in doctrine and Christian spirituality.

What are we supposed to *do* with this creed? As a document of confessional theology, the creed is helpful and edifying, and we can grow in our appreciation and understanding of Nicene theology, but what next? What is the function of the creed? The Nicene Creed does not address everything proper to the Christian life, but it does offer what is necessary for Christian belief: faith in the person and work of Jesus Christ and the triune God. The creed does not come with an instruction manual for its application, though it is undoubtedly a manual for instruction. The earliest receivers of the creed used it in their individual and corporate lives. The creed was first applied to (1) written theological declarations and (2) liturgical uses in baptism and church services.[1]

While we do not cover all the uses of the creed in the early church, we highlight several ways in which the creed was used in church life for spiritual edification.[2] Primarily, the creed served as a foundation for baptismal preparation. It was also used for catechesis, sermons, daily spirituality, and much more. Beyond regularly reciting the creed, we hope modern Christians consider the various ways that Christians throughout history have used the creed to build up and edify the church.

The Nicene Creed for Baptism

Think back to your baptism experience. Those in the free-church tradition typically emphasize baptism based on a personal confession of Christ as Lord and the testimony of salvation. Maybe

---

[1] Wolfram Kinzig, *A History of Early Christian Creeds* (De Gruyter, 2024), 406.

[2] See Kinzig, *Early Christian Creeds*; Wolfram Kinzig, ed., *Faith in Formulae: A Collection of Early Christian Creeds and Creed-Related Texts*, 4 vols., Oxford Early Christian Texts (Oxford University Press, 2017).

your experience of baptism included a brief recounting of your conversion to those gathered. Or perhaps you responded to a spontaneous call for baptism at a church, camp, or other Christian event. Some are baptized in a very public manner, and others at an intimate family gathering. For better or worse, the free-church tradition has emphasized the preparation and practice of baptism in different ways, so that baptismal candidates have varying experiences. Spontaneous baptism, or baptism without some period of instruction, did not exist as a category in the mind of the ancient Christian.

The predominant function of the Nicene Creed in the early church was as a baptismal confession. Catechumens—those who had been taught the tenets of the faith in preparation for baptism and church membership—recited the Nicene Creed as a statement of Christian identity and confession. The creed was also used in a *declarative* or *interrogative* sense at the baptismal event; the participant either verbally recited the creed or responded to questions from the bishop about their Christian belief based on the creed.

Scholars have offered different theories about how the Nicene Creed was formulated. Some theorize that a local baptismal creed used by Eusebius of Caesarea served as the theological foundation for the Nicene Creed. Eusebius introduces his creed: "As we have received from the bishops who preceded us, in our first catechesis, and when we received baptism; and as we have learned from the divine Scriptures; and as we constantly believed and taught as a presbyter and now as bishop, so also believing at the time present, we report to our faith."[3] Although he provides his own version of

---

[3] Eusebius, *Epistula ad ecclesiam Caesariensem*. Translated in Kinzig, *Early Christian Creeds*, 235.

the creed, in it Eusebius articulates the public faith taught by the bishops and confessed by catechumens.

Rufinus of Aquileia commented on the role of creedal confessions and baptism. He refers to the use of the Apostles' Creed in the Latin Church: "The ancient custom is maintained there whereby candidates who are on the point of receiving the grace of baptism deliver the creed publicly, in the hearing of the congregation of the faithful. As a result, since those who have preceded them in the faith are listening attentively, the interpolation of even a single article is not tolerated."[4] Rufinus aligns himself with a tradition that preceded his ministry: baptismal candidates audibly and publicly recited the rule of faith (in this case, the Apostles' Creed) before their baptism. Part of this practice was for the Christian community to hear the confession of faith and determine the validity of their baptism. At the Council of Laodicea (363–364), churches were instructed: "They who are to be baptized must learn the faith [creed] by heart, and recite it to the bishop, or to the presbyters, on the fifth day of the week."[5] We assume that you did not have to memorize the creed nor recite it to the pastor before your baptism; neither did we. This is out of step with the witness and practice of the early church.

In the first centuries of the church, the creed was both declarative and interrogative in baptism. Men and women entering the waters of baptism were prepared to answer questions about their beliefs based on the creed, and the bishop asked the candidates whether they believed in each of its articles. The *Old Gelasian Sacramentary* (*c.* 750) demonstrates an example of an interrogative baptismal liturgy. Scholars affirm that some of the material in this work can be dated as far back as AD 150:

---

[4] Rufinus, *A Commentary on the Apostles' Creed,* 3.

[5] Council of Laodicea, canon 46.

> Then, after the blessing of the fount, you baptize everyone in turn, using these interrogations: "Do you believe in God, the Father Almighty?"
>
> He answers, "I believe."
>
> "Do you believe in Jesus Christ, his own Son, our Lord, [who was] born and suffered?"
>
> He answers, "I believe."
>
> "Do you also believe in the Holy Spirit, the holy Church, the remission of sins, the resurrection of the flesh?"
>
> He answers, "I believe."
>
> Then each time you immerse him thrice in the water.[6]

In this scenario, each person is baptized, one at a time, and is immersed three times according to the trinitarian persons. While form differed slightly in each community, the consistent formula of creedal recitation for baptism remained the same. The creed established the boundary of the Christian faith and shaped the shared confession of catechumens as they entered the church.

The Creed for the Eucharist

The Nicene Creed served as the theological nerve center of Christian theology, providing the spiritual impulses necessary to animate the church and its teaching. The creed continued as a declaration of the church's faith, a pledge of allegiance to continually affirm the commitment to the triune God of redemption.

---

[6] Kinzig, *Early Christian Creeds*, 122.

The creed was used in the church in the western empire to prepare for the Eucharist celebration possibly as early as the time of Ambrose of Milan (c. 339–397). Ambrose, for example, once dismissed the catechumens from the service altogether. They reviewed the creed before their baptism and were incorporated into the body of Christ to participate in the Eucharist service.[7] However, as evidence tentatively suggests, "the creed was not introduced into the liturgy of the eucharist in the eastern part of the empire until the fifth or sixth century."[8] Maximus the Confessor indicated that the creed was recited before the celebration of the Eucharist and *after* the doors had been closed, excluding the unbaptized and catechumenate.[9]

In the liturgies of Basil, Gregory of Nazianzus, and John Chrysostom, the creed is stated during the Eucharist services. In the liturgy of Gregory, the congregation confesses before the Eucharist: "I believe, I believe, I believe and confess to the last breath that this is the life-giving flesh of your only-begotten Son, our Lord, God, and Saviour Jesus Christ."[10] Whereas the Nicene Creed was not confessed verbatim, its contents appear in the pre-Eucharistic liturgy. The liturgies of Basil and Chrysostom present the creedal recitation as the first event of the Eucharist service.[11]

Several early Christian churches offered different services with different functions. Closed doors indicated an exclusionary Eucharist service. Once the community, specifically the bishops, confirmed the testimony and commitment of a person, he or she

---

[7] Ambrose, *Epistle* 76, 4; See also Kinzig, *Early Christian Creeds*, 487–88.

[8] Kinzig, *Early Christian Creeds*, 507.

[9] *Mystagogia* 15.

[10] *Faith in Formula* §694a.

[11] *Faith in Formula* §694b.

would be catechized and then baptized. This practice demonstrates the shepherding function of the creed. In this sense, the creed was exclusionary, marking out confirmed believers from those who have not yet entered the church, through baptism and participation in the Eucharist. After this creedal confirmation, church members could partake of the "holy things"—the Eucharistic elements of bread and wine. In the liturgy of Saint Mark, the community recited the creedal confession while standing.[12]

Other theologians testify to a similar tradition. For example, Isidore of Seville records that the creed was "proclaimed by the congregation at the time of sacrifice [i.e., Eucharist]."[13] Isidore argues, "This rule of the true faith excels in such doctrinal mysteries that it speaks about every part of the faith . . . It crushes all the errors of impiety and the blasphemies of faithfulness and because of this it is proclaimed in a matching confession by the congregation in all the churches."[14] Today, we rarely credit a creed or confession with this sort of power in the believer's life, because we forget the formative power of verbal declarations coupled with heartfelt faith. Declaring our faith aloud reinforces what we believe and further seals it on our hearts.

The Creed for Catechesis

As a marker and confession of Christian identity, the Nicene Creed is also used for theological instruction. Catechesis, or teaching, in the faith is a process that helps would-be church members understand the basics of the Christian worldview, the biblical narrative, and the necessary components of Christian theological reflection.

[12] *Faith in Formula* §692.

[13] *De ecclesiasticis officiis* I, 16.

[14] *De ecclesiasticis officiis* I, 16.

It initiates discipleship, giving new believers and truth seekers a new, biblical conceptualization of reality before their total commitment to Christ via baptism. Another use of the Nicene Creed (and of the Old Roman Creed and the Apostles' Creed) is as a theological confession of the essential Christian beliefs. Confessing the Nicene Creed is synonymous with confessing the Christian faith, while denial of the Nicene faith is contrary to Christian belief. We remember a conversation with a theological mentor of ours who stated, "If someone is unable to recite and believe the Nicene Creed, I must doubt whether they are a Christian."

In an example from the fifth century, Saint Cyril of Alexandria presents the creed as foundational for the universal Christian theological confession; he used the creed to expel Nestorius and considered him outside the Christian faith. For Cyril, it is not only necessary to confess the creed but to interpret the creed correctly: "But it shall not suffice for your reverence [Nestorius] to confess with us just the profession of the faith set forth in the Holy Spirit during critical times by the holy and great synod assembled in the city of Nicaea. You have not understood and have not interpreted it rightly, but rather perversely, even if you confess the text with your lips."[15] Cyril notes the universal application of this creed: "For this is the faith of the Catholic and Apostolic Church to which all the orthodox bishops throughout the West and East agree."[16] The Nicene Creed is structural to Christian theology and identity, but it is also polemical and pastoral. Those who claim to be Christian ought to be tested by their belief and adherence to the doctrinal content contained within the creed.

The creed is a memorable orthodox statement for all Christians. The Third Council of Constantinople (680–81) recognized it as

[15] Cyril of Alexandria, *ep.* 17.5.

[16] Cyril of Alexandria, *ep.* 17.6.

the orthodox faith: "This pious and orthodox Symbol of the divine grace sufficed for both the full knowledge and the confirmation of the orthodox faith."[17] Augustine notes how the creed is structured to encourage memorization: "So the Symbol is a briefly compiled rule of faith, intended to instruct the mind without overburdening the memory; to be said in a few words, from which much is to be gained."[18] Augustine remarks also on its brevity: "But they have been compressed into a brief summary, and reduced to a definite, tightly knit order; and that is how they are to be handed over to you, to build up your faith and to prepare you to confess it, without burdening your memories."[19] The creed's short, definitive statements of faith reverberate with biblical truth and their brevity eases the burden of memorization.

Early converts to the Christian faith were catechized with the creed to ensure their confession of the faith. Bishops, too, wrote commentaries on the creed to aid their spiritual community. In *Epistle* 125, Basil of Caesarea recalls a man who formerly held to a non-Nicene confession but then entered the orthodox tradition: "Those who previously held to some other confession of faith and now wish to change over to the congregation of the orthodox and also those who now desire to be instructed in the teaching of the doctrine of truth for the first time, must be taught the creed written by the blessed fathers in the council which was previously assembled at Nicaea."[20] For people new to the faith or transferring membership from a church out of step with orthodoxy, the creed was used didactically to ensure the confession of proper doctrine before baptism or reception into the church.

---

[17] *Faith in Formula* §242c.

[18] Augustine, *Sermon* 213.2.

[19] Augustine, *Sermon* 214.1.

[20] Basil, *ep.* 125.1.

Another common practice was to prohibit the catechumens from writing down the creed while memorizing it. This was to aid the memory and the implanting of the creed in the hearts of new converts. As Augustine asserts, "You are to learn it thoroughly by hearing it, and not write it down either when you have it by heart, but keep it always and go over it in your memory."[21] In the spirit of Jer 31:33, Augustine expects the Holy Spirit to write the "Symbol" (creed) on the person's heart. Augustine uses the language of "handing over" or "giving back" the creed: Eight days after receiving it from the Bishops, the catechumens would audibly confess the creed.[22]

The Creed for Daily Spiritual Life

Caesarius of Arles (c. 470–542) often encouraged the congregation to memorize and recite the creed for their spiritual life. For example, in *Sermon* 6, he makes a lesser-to-greater argument: If pagans recite love songs that produce what the devil teaches, ought not Christians be able to memorize what Christ has revealed? He suggests that the Nicene Creed, the Lord's Prayer, and various songs and psalms should be learned and regularly recited so that believers might "join their soul to God and liberate it from the devil."[23] Caesarius further suggests that the creed should be learned in the context of the family: "Preserve the creed and the Lord's Prayer yourself, and teach it to your children, for I do not know how someone who refuses to learn the few lines of the creed and the Lord's Prayer could be so bold as to call himself a Christian."[24] Just as modern Christians often pray before a car trip, Caesarius

---

[21] Augustine, *Sermon* 212.2.

[22] Augustine, *Sermon* 213.11.

[23] *Sermon* 6, 3.

[24] *Sermon* 13, 2.

suggests reciting the Lord's Prayer and the creed while traveling: "But anytime you need to hurry along somewhere, sign yourself in the name of Christ, reciting the creed and the Lord's Prayer faithfully, carry on with your journey, protected by God's help."[25]

In the Shema (Deut 6:4–9; 11:13–21; Num 15:37–41), God commands Israel to teach that the Lord is one when one rises, when one sits down, and as one goes along the way. The church received similar instruction concerning the creed. For example, Augustine exhorts Christians to memorize the creed in church to then be able to recite it daily. Augustine offers the creed as the new *shema*:

> You see, if you haven't got the creed by heart now, you don't hear the creed every day in church, in the assembled people. But when you have it by heart, say it every day, in order not to forget it. When you get up, when you go to bed, give back your creed, give it back to the Lord, remind yourselves of it, don't be tired of repeating it. Repetition is a good thing, to prevent forgetfulness creeping in. Don't say, "I said it yesterday, I said it today, I say it every day, I know it well and truly by heart." Call your faith to mind, look at yourself; treat your creed as your own personal mirror. Observe yourself there, if you believe all the things you confess to believing, and rejoice every day in your faith.[26]

A fourth-century bishop, Nicetas of Remesiana, encouraged people to memorize the creed and to speak it daily to themselves:

> Indeed everyone desirous of attaining unto faith and baptism is to be instructed fully concerning the faith, as is

[25] *Sermon* 54, 1.

[26] *Sermon* 58, 13. See also Augustine, *Sermon to Catechumens on the Creed* 1, 1; *Sermon* 215, 1.

> contained in this same creed, and likewise to be taught that he should keep memorized in his heart the brevity of the faith by speaking it to himself daily: before he goes to sleep, when he awakes from sleep, [and] by bearing it in mind at all times.[27]

Caesarius argues that the whole household should be taught the creed: "Above all teach not only your children but your entire household to memorize the creed, because, if a man does not arrange for his household to learn the creed, he shows himself to be a tepid and negligent Christian."[28] According to these examples, the creedal recitation should occupy a person's routine and daily rituals. Imagine if you recited the Lord's Prayer every day for a week. What would this activity do to your spiritual life? Some of the earliest Christians recited the Lord's Prayer three times a day (Did. 8.3). Now imagine reciting the prayer and the creed together every day for a week. What would this activity do to your spiritual and theological formation?

The Creed for Corporate Recitation

We are happy to hear of churches within the free-church tradition using the creed in corporate worship. Throughout the development of the church's liturgy of time, the placement of the creed within the church service changed, signifying differing functions of the creed. Regardless of placement in the liturgy, the creed has been vital to the worshipping church since its inception. Kinzig offers four functions worth mentioning:

---

[27] *De gentilitatis erroribus* II, 2.

[28] *Sermon* 130, 5.

1. The *catechumenate instruction* of the creed prepared new Christians for baptism.
2. The *liturgical recitation* of the creed preceded the participation in the Eucharist.
3. The *theological litmus* of the creed verified the salvation, baptism, and orthodox faith of a person participating in the Eucharist.
4. The *corporate response* of the creed made up the church's proper response to the Gospel that concluded the liturgy of the Word.[29]

In addition, we briefly show how the creed was used in corporate singing and preaching. There are many other ways the creed can be incorporated into the life of the local church, and we encourage you to consider meaningful ways to use the creed and its content to edify and build up the body.[30]

In Corporate Recitation and Singing

Songwriting and singing have been part of Christianity since its inception. We see an early and practical use for Nicene theology in the pro-Nicene hymns of Ambrose of Milan and Ephraem Syrus. As far as we understand, the Nicene Creed itself was never considered a poetic text, let alone song lyrics. The Apostles' Creed continued to serve as a baptismal catechesis; the Nicene Creed "was seen as a solemn declaration of faith to be chanted in mass

---

[29] Whereas we offer the wording and summaries, we depend upon the findings and summaries of Kinzig. See Kinzig, *Early Christian Creeds*, 515.

[30] For more perspective and ideas on how the Nicene Creed was used historically, see Kinzig, *Early Christian Creeds*, 518–22.

on Sundays and major festivals where it usually functioned as 'the conclusion of the reading service, the joyous "yes" of the faithful to the message they received.'"[31] However, there are a few recorded instances when the creed was recited and sung by corporate gatherings.

As alluded to before, there were at least two services of the corporate gathering: liturgy of the Word and liturgy of the Eucharist. In the liturgy of the Eucharist, the congregation recited the creed after the greeting and before the Lord's Prayer and the Eucharist. John of Biclaro was both a bishop and chronicler in the sixth and seventh centuries. He reflects that the Creed of Constantinople (a reiteration and expansion of the Nicene Creed written in 381), "which had been laudably accepted at the Council of Chalcedon," was "sung together by the congregation," before the Lord's Prayer.[32] The Third Council of Toledo (589) is known for adding the *filioque* ("and from the Son") clause to the Niceno-Constantinople Creed in the church of the western empire. However, canon 2 of Toledo mentions that the creed is to be sung by the congregation before the Lord's Prayer during Eucharist liturgies:

> In all the churches of Spain and Gaul or Galicia, the creed of the Council of Constantinople, that is, of the 150 bishops, be recited according to the convention of the Eastern churches so that, before the Lord's Prayer is said, the creed shall be proclaimed [*or* chanted] aloud by the congregation. By this let the true faith bear clear testimony and also, the

[31] Kinzig, *Early Christian Creeds*, 572. The partial quotation is from Josef A. Jungmann, *The Mass of the Roman Rite: Its Origins and Development* (Benziger, 1951), I:471.

[32] John of Biclaro, *Chronicon* 2. See also Kinzig, *Early Christian Creeds*, 510.

> people's hearts having been cleaned by the faith, let them draw near to partake of the body and blood of Christ.[33]

In Preaching

Alongside singing or chanting, attention to the preaching of the creed emerged. For example, Ambrose,[34] Augustine,[35] and Peter Chrysologus preached sermons about the creed.[36] In the sixth century, Gregory the Great provided a fervent and timeless charge to preachers: "For with an entirely pure conscience we preach, hold, and defend to the last drop of our blood that faith which has been handed down by the apostles, was preserved inviolate by their successors, and was taken up and rendered into a creed by the revered Nicene Council of the 318 fathers."[37] Modern preachers, too, must adhere to the truth with a pure conscience and defend the apostolic gospel message poignantly articulated at Nicaea.

In *Sermon* 212, Augustine commends what he calls the "Symbol," "in which is briefly contained everything that is believed for the sake of eternal salvation."[38] The creed is often described as a "Symbol" in early Christian literature. Everything in the Symbol "is already contained in the divine documents of the holy scriptures."[39] Symbols, according to Augustine, are used in commercial transactions, "which guarantee their loyalty to the terms of their association.

---

[33] *Faith in Formula* §687b.

[34] Ambrose, *Explanatio symboli.*

[35] Augustine, *Sermons* 212–215; *On Faith and the Creed*; *A Sermon to Catechumens on the Creed.*

[36] Peter Chrysologus, *Sermons* 56–62.

[37] *Faith in Formula* §367.

[38] *Sermon* 212.1.

[39] *Sermon* 212.2.

And your association is concerned with spiritual merchandise."[40] The Symbol, therefore, designates commitment and identity: "The reason it is called a symbol is that in it is contained the prescribed faith and pledge of our association, and it is by confessing it, as by giving a password, that the faithful Christian can be recognized."[41]

As Augustine affirms, no one can be saved unless they first believe. Only after calling on the Lord can one receive the Symbol of faith.[42] After eight days, the hearers (most likely catechumens) then "give back" what they have received by publicly reciting the creed.[43] Early in Augustine's ministry, he interpreted Rom 10:9–10 as referring to the Symbol: "This is what the Symbol builds up in you, what you must both believe and confess, so that you may be saved. And indeed, the things you are going to receive in a short enough form, to be committed to memory and repeated by word of mouth, are not new things which you haven't heard before. I mean, you are quite used to hearing them in the holy scriptures and in sermons in church."[44]

Augustine preached the creed to encourage young pastors and new Christians. He confessed, "I will do my best, for the love I have for you, to the extent that my age and my inexperience allow, and the fact that I am only a new recruit in the office I have been entrusted with."[45] We learn this from Augustine: The creed is a helpful pastoral tool for both the new and the seasoned pastor. Pastors should see the creed as their biblical guide for teaching, preaching, counseling, and leading others to the life-giving Word of God.

---

[40] *Sermon* 212.1.

[41] *Sermon* 214.12.

[42] *Sermon* 213.1.

[43] *Sermon* 213.11.

[44] *Sermon* 214.1.

[45] *Sermon* 214.1.

Biblical Connections

The divine injunction in Deuteronomy 6 provides an Old Testament precedent for repeated, creedal instruction. We must love and cherish God's law from the heart, but to do so requires diligent instruction and recitation. God's people are to confess that the Lord is God, and he is one (v. 4). God's people are to love the Lord with their heart, soul, and strength (v. 5). God's people must repeat this command to their children and talk about it when they sit and when they walk (Deut 6:7). It should both symbolically and literally adorn their homes and lives (vv. 8–9). J. A. Thompson observes, "The demand of love towards God implies all other demands, and the disposition to love God implies the disposition both to obey his commandments and to impart these to the children of the following generations, so as to maintain an attitude of love and obedience among the people of God from age to age."[46] Eugene Merrill adds, "The image is that of the engraver of a monument who takes hammer and chisel in hand and with painstaking care etches a text into the face of a solid slab of granite. The sheer labor of such a task is daunting indeed, but once done the message is there to stay."[47] We must chisel the truth of God into our hearts and the hearts of the covenant community of faith. Though the new covenant in Christ guarantees that God's law resides in our hearts (see Jer 31:33), we are not exempt from diligently imparting the faith.

Another aspect of Deuteronomy 6 is the picture of "talking" and "walking" in the Word of God. The task of teaching is active.

---

[46] J. A. Thompson, *Deuteronomy: An Introduction and Commentary*, Tyndale Old Testament Commentaries 5 (IVP, 1974), 139.

[47] Eugene H. Merrill, *Deuteronomy*, The New American Commentary 4 (B&H, 1994), 167.

We do not merely download divine data into a brain, but by teaching we shape human hearts to love the Lord. God's people are to walk and talk about him actively. In confessing God's existence and lordship, and loving him with our whole self, we must also engage in the challenging yet beautiful daily task of talking about him and walking with one another. This requires careful attention to sound theology, deep discipleship, and practices for spiritual formation.[48] It also requires us to be aware of what happened at Nicaea in 325. While the command to walk and talk revolves around the content of God's revelation, it also requires creativity to help Christians and would-be disciples grow in their understanding and conviction of the truth. Nicaea and similar creedal statements are a biblically sanctioned way to help God's people "walk" and "talk" about the God they adore. The creed orients our instruction, liturgies, preaching, and daily spiritual life toward our confession of the truth about God and toward our love for him. While Moses likely did not foresee the Council of Nicaea, his instructions to God's people in Deuteronomy set the precedent for walking and talking in our love for the Lord. From the great creeds to orthodox confessions of faith to commentary literature and devotional material, the church seeks to be faithful to the vision and instruction of Deuteronomy 6. We should fruitfully use each way to talk and walk for the building up of God's people, and aim to impart the faith and commands of God to each generation.

---

[48] We have been shaped by the proposal to prioritize making theologically aware disciples in the local church given by J. T. English, *Deep Discipleship: How the Church Can Make Whole Disciples of Jesus* (B&H, 2020). To further explore a practical understanding of theological and practical categories of spiritual formation, see Coleman M. Ford, *Formed in His Image: A Guide for Christian Formation* (B&H, 2023).

Conclusion

The Nicene Creed is not a cold and static statement but a biblically charged tool meant to fuel discipleship and worship. It provides doctrine to learn, statements to recite, phrases to sing, and content to preach. For pastors, it provides a stable framework for a ministry of teaching and preaching founded on God's word. For theologians, it gives the paradigm by which we articulate theological systems and propositions. For every Christian, the creed is the buttress to our commitment to Christ as Lord and the lens through which we read Scripture and articulate our faith. The creed should have a place in every Bible-believing church as a tool for worship and discipleship. The early church testifies that the creed is our precious resource for our edification and sanctification. It can never replace the Bible, but it should be used to understand the Word better. To jettison this timeless standard of faith is to all but scrap the Christian faith entirely. May it never be!

CHAPTER 8

No Creed but the Bible? How the Nicene Creed Explains the Bible

[The Son is] begotten, not made, consubstantial with the Father, "through whom all things came to be" (John 1:3), both the things in heaven and the things on earth.

—The Nicene Creed (325)

For everything was created by him, in heaven and on earth, the visible and the invisible, whether thrones or dominions or rulers or authorities—all things have been created through him and for him.

—Colossians 1:16

Thinking Nicenely Today: There is a right way and a wrong way to read the Bible. The Nicene Creed gives the church a time-tested, biblically faithful, theologically accurate guide for reading, interpreting, and spiritually benefiting from Scripture. Insofar as the church reads the Bible correctly and profitably, we do so in accordance with the Nicene Creed.

Having looked at the historical, theological, and liturgical contexts of the creed, there is a lot we can now say about how the creed can help us today. In chapter 7, we argue for the thoughtful use of the creed in the worshipping life of the church. However, we also advocate for the creed as *the* guide for reading and understanding Scripture. We must read the Nicene Creed theologically, with our Bible in mind. We read the creed as a living voice, while reading Scripture, considering theological formulation, and teaching Christian theology in the church. We can read the Scriptures in the twenty-first century and assume the theological framework of Nicaea. Simply put, the Nicene Creed is a faithful guide for scriptural exegesis. We give two suggestions for reading the Nicene Creed alongside the Scriptures: (1) assume a Nicene trinitarian framework when speaking of God (*theology*) and God's activity in the world (*economy*), and (2) read Christological Scripture passages according to the Christological article (as discussed in chapters 3 and 4) and the Son's two natures (i.e., partitive exegesis).

Reading Nicenely for Spiritual Benefit

The trinitarian debates of the fourth century included early Christian appropriations of philosophy and were primarily about Scripture and theology. Scriptural exegesis was the main concern for theologians amid fourth-century debates. Lewis Ayres observes:

> Particular exegetical questions were central to the debates, even as those texts and debates had generated questions that Christians had long approached by adapting to their use of non-Christian philosophical doctrines and modes of thinking. Indeed, the fourth-century debates were themselves dependent on modes of arguing philosophically

> about scriptural texts that Christians had been shaping since the early second century.[1]

Mark Edwards adds, "When Christians of the fourth century undertook to defend the Nicene Creed by philosophical reasoning, the terms of greatest moment to them were *ousia* and *dunamis* ('being' and 'power' or 'potentiality') . . . To Christians they were scriptural, but the meanings grafted onto them by all parties to theological controversies in this epoch, are derived, by way of Plotinus and Porphyry."[2] Those who confess the eternal generation of the Son—the One who descended from heaven to earth by taking on human nature, who suffered, was crucified, and died, was buried, resurrected, and ascended—engage with scriptural exegesis and the eternal mystery of God. This discussion does not disregard philosophy, but hones it with the proper biblical qualifications to exemplify the true sense of the Word of God.

Thus, the theology of Nicaea provides us a way of reading Scripture *nicenely*, according to the principles and content of the creed. Thinking per the Nicene Creed also consists of a culture of reading per Nicene theology; the two mutually reinforce one another. The Fathers of the church generally read Scripture within a relationship between theological commitments and the spiritual life. In this way, scriptural exegesis includes not only *how* someone reads Scripture but the entire culture of one's theological and spiritual commitments. Andrew Louth reflects on the relationship of early Christian theology and scriptural exegesis: "If the results that the historical-critical method yields when applied to Scripture

---

[1] Lewis Ayres, "Scripture in the Trinitarian Controversies," in *The Oxford Handbook of Early Christian Biblical Interpretation*, ed. Paul M. Blowers and Peter W. Martens (Oxford University Press, 2019), 439.

[2] Mark Edwards, *Aristotle and Early Christian Thought*, Studies in Philosophy and Theology in Late Antiquity (Routledge, 2019), 78–79.

are too meagre, maybe we shall do better if we include the creeds, the councils, and the Fathers. But it is not clear that the ground is then all that much more secure: for the Fathers, and creeds, and councils claim to be interpreting Scripture. How can one accept their results if one does not accept their methods?"[3] The theological vision drawn from Nicaea impacts scriptural exegesis and supports ancient theological presuppositions. Reading *nicenely* means appreciating a premodern exegetical vision, which leads to a more spiritually enriching reading of Scripture.

The scheme known as partitive exegesis (the focus of this chapter) is one way of reading Scripture that accords with Nicene Christology and correctly relates the Word to the persons of the triune God and the two natures of Christ. It adds, rather than detracts, from the spiritual formation of the Christian. That said, not all models of *partitive exegesis* assume the theological movements of pro-Nicene theology. As we seek to demonstrate, sound theological exegesis assumes the background of Nicene history and pro-Nicene theological development.

We provide three related definitions of partitive exegesis. Each definition progressively builds on the previous one(s) to add layers of (necessary) complexity and help us grasp how we read Scripture using categories gleaned from Nicene theology.

> (Stage 1: Beginning Thesis) Partitive exegesis is a way to read Scripture *nicenely* with Nicene pressures.
>
> (Stage 2: Intermediate Thesis) Partitive exegesis is a way to read Scripture, particularly passages about the Son, that assumes the threefold framework of Philippians 2 and

---

[3] Andrew Louth, *Discerning the Mystery: An Essay on the Nature of Theology* (Clarendon, 1983), 100.

> Nicene Christology; it identifies the two natures of the Son (divine and human), considers the entire career of the Son (eternal, incarnate, exalted), and admits the divine mystery about the incarnation.
>
> (Stage 3: Advanced Thesis) Partitive exegesis is a way to read Scripture that assumes the metaphysics and mystery of a two-natured single Son (divine and human natures), situates the entire career of the Son according to Philippians 2 and Nicene Christology (divine and human activities), prohibits univocal readings of the Scriptures about the Son and two natures (*communication of idioms*), and places Scripture reading within a *theology-economy* framework.

We intentionally use the term "Nicene pressure" to describe our scriptural exegesis. "Biblical pressure" is a term coined by Kavin Rowe, who builds on the thought of Brevard Childs.[4] Childs assumes that "traditional Christian exegesis understood its theological reflection to be responding to the coercion or pressure of the biblical text itself."[5] From this premise, Rowe argues, "The biblical text is not inert but instead exerts a pressure, or 'coercion,' upon its interpreters and asserts itself within theological reflection and discourse such that there is (or can be) a profound continuity, grounded in the subject matter itself, between the biblical text and traditional Christian exegesis and theological formulation."[6] In other words, "biblical pressure" causes the interpreter to make

[4] C. Kavin Rowe, "Biblical Pressure and Trinitarian Hermeneutics," *Pro Ecclesia* 11, no. 3 (2002): 295–312; Brevard S. Childs, "Toward Recovering Theological Exegesis," *Pro Ecclesia* 6, no. 1 (1997): 16–26.

[5] Childs, "Theological Exegesis," 17.

[6] Rowe, "Trinitarian Hermeneutics," 308.

certain judgments about the text. It also points beyond the text when speaking about scriptural and doctrinal implications. With this concept and the three stages in mind, we will explore how Scripture and the creed interact for biblical interpretation and theological discourse.

Creed and Scripture: Foundations for Partitive Exegesis

In the biblical and theological blueprint, all things come from God—the Trinity—and God serves as the starting point for reflection on Scripture and creed. All things find their proper order when God serves as the first principle. We agree with John Webster that "principles" are foundational elements of knowledge or "those realities and powers by virtue of which other things exist and can be known."[7] Our concept of creation, Scripture, the church, and more begin with God's eternal existence. God is, therefore, we are. Scripture is derivative of God and serves as a sufficient communicative act of God's eternal being. Thus, the act of "theology" or "theological reflection" fits within the economy of God as people receive grace, use intellectual capacities, and reflect (imperfectly) on Scripture. Again, Webster helps us here: "Christian theology is reason's recognition, contemplation and articulation of this divine wisdom ministered to us by these servants of God."[8] Scriptural interpretation is an act of imperfect theological reflection; because we have limited abilities, we pursue Christian theology as

---

[7] John Webster, *God Without Measure: Working Papers in Christian Theology, Volume II: Virtue and Intellect*, T&T Clark Theology (Bloomsbury, 2016), 142.

[8] John Webster, *The Domain of the Word: Scripture and Theological Reason*, T&T Clark Theology (Bloomsbury, 2012), x.

contemplation of God by the help of God in service to the people of God.

By recognizing God as the ultimate good, that Scripture comes from God, and theology is derivative from Scripture, we see how the church may profitably use the Nicene Creed in the economy of God's activity in the world. Without oversimplifying this process, we enumerate the affirmations necessary for theological reflection, with a measure of *apophaticism* (attention to divine mystery), to show how to read Scripture *nicenely*:

> The eternal triune God (1) self-exists within himself, (2) self-reveals through both the visible Word (the eternal Son made flesh) and the communicative acts of revelation (Scripture, creation, and the sacraments),[9] and (3) invites his image bearers to participate in his life through conversion and communion with God.
>
> The church (4) imperfectly and partially reflects on God's communicative acts to envision the life and practice of a Christian and (5) will perfectly and fully envision God's eternal being and happily dwell with God in heaven.

To read *nicenely*, we must know how God, Scripture, and creed properly relate. Scripture is an infallible record of God's

---

[9] Our use of "sacrament" here refers to how the acts of Baptism and Eucharist (or Lord's Supper) are the unique ordinances through which the gospel is visibly displayed and spiritually signified to the Church. See Michael Haykin, *Amidst Us Our Beloved Stands: Recovering Sacrament in the Baptist Tradition* (Lexham, 2022). See also Coleman M. Ford, *Formed in His Image: A Guide for Christian Formation* (B&H, 2023), 123–26. See also Coleman M. Ford and Shawn J. Wilhite, *Ancient Wisdom for the Care of Souls: Learning the Art of Pastoral Ministry from the Church Fathers* (Crossway, 2024).

communicative act. The creed is the church's fallible reflection on God's infallible activity. This does not mean the creed is invalid or without authority, but its authority and usefulness derive from Scripture. The creed is the church's reckoning of the biblical narrative and reflection on the incarnation, deployed in idiomatic phrases to aid memorization, recitation, and embodiment. Scriptural exegesis and interpretation is not on par with the authority of Scripture but is the church's imperfect activity of reflection on God. Webster notes that "theology has its controlling center in exegesis of Holy Scripture; Holy Scripture is the Word of God; the Word of God summons us to faithful reading."[10] He reflects elsewhere that "[t]he Creed is a good servant but a bad master."[11] Therefore, the church uses the creed to gain biblical and theological clarity regarding the triune God and his acts.

Rightly ordering Scripture and creed assists the church in contemplating God. Before explaining the relationship between the Bible and the Nicene Creed, we need to affirm the following two statements:

1. Scripture is from God, through the Son, in the Spirit, and for the church. Scripture, irrespective of interpretation, is derived from God's divine mind, and is the triune God's self-disclosure to humanity for redemption, communion, and delight.

[10] John Webster, *The Culture of Theology*, ed. Ivor J. Davidson and Alden C. McCray (Baker Academic, 2019), 65.

[11] John Webster, "Confession and Confessions," in *Nicene Christianity: The Future for a New Ecumenism*, ed. Christopher R. Seitz (Brazos Press, 2001), 120.

2. The creed derives from Scripture through reflection by the Spirit-empowered church. Ecumenical creeds, as they present biblical truth, are derived through the Spirit's work in the church's imperfect reflection of God's communicative acts. Thus, a Creed summarizes the Spirit's revelation of the Scriptures to the church.

By understanding the nature of Scripture and the creed, we are better positioned to engage in biblical interpretation and theological discourse. Because Scripture is from God, we must not confuse our interpretations as revelations from God. Our biblical reasoning occurs within the economy of God, through the help of the Spirit, and within the locale of the church. Thus, our interpretation ought to be shaped by grace, patience, love, hope, gentleness, and joy so that the people of God can love God more deeply and love their neighbor more completely. Since Scripture is from God, its source is God, who is ultimately incomprehensible. As interpretation occurs within the church, it is limited by human finitude in need of continual moral transformation. Yet, we can still affirm the worthy goal of the early church's creedal formation as an exercise in theological discourse and scriptural reflection. Creeds and confessions arise throughout history to shape and sharpen the church's worship. The Nicene Creed is a derivative authority based on the church's reflection of Scripture; it is scriptural but not Scripture. It is a trustworthy guide and framework for exegesis because its content attests to the infallible source himself: God.

To show the relationship between Scripture and Creed, we reflect on Philippians 2 as it informs the creedal affirmations of Christ's person and work. Here, we unpack the schema of the Son's life (eternal, incarnate, and exalted) as conveyed by the apostle Paul and coordinate those statements to the creed.

Table 1: Philippians 2 and the Nicene Creed

Eternal Son: "in the form of God"	**Incarnate Son: "taking on the form of a servant"**	**Exalted Son: "God has highly exalted him"**
One Nature: Fully Divine	Two Natures: Fully Divine and Fully Human	Two Natures: Fully Divine and Glorified Humanity
"who was begotten from the Father before all ages": Eternal Generation	"he descended and became incarnate": The Human Birth of the Divine Son	"[He] ascended into the heavens": The Ascension of Christ
"God from God, Light from Light": Eternally Shared Properties (*X of X*)	"was crucified, [and] suffered": The Death and Work of Christ	"is seated at the right hand": The Rule and Reign of Christ
Eternal Activities in the Divine Life	"was buried": The Mystery of Holy Saturday	"is coming again with glory": The Return and Reign of Christ
"through whom all things came to be": Eternal Activities toward Creation	"rose on the third day": The Resurrection of Christ	"whose kingdom will have no end": Eternal Kingdom of God

Using the Nicene Creed alongside the Philippian Hymn (Phil 2:6–11), we may speak about the Son before creation and before his incarnation, the Son's incarnation and human life (especially using the four Gospels), and the heavenly and future realities of the Son. In this small but theologically significant passage, we see how Scripture establishes a pattern for creedal affirmations, mirroring the pattern and content given at Nicaea.

The Language of *Theology* and *Economy*

Showing how the creed and the Bible relate, we offer a brief proposal on speaking about God *nicenely*. Here, we use the terms theology (*theologia*) and economy (*oikonomia*) and provide distinct points to consider regarding their proper usage.

Whereas some modern theologians use the language of "immanent" and "economic," we suggest moving away from those terms to affirm *theology-economy* language. Alongside theologians such as Fred Sanders and Gilles Emery, we believe the immanent-economic framework does not cohere well with the pro-Nicene model of *theology-economy.* Our proposal includes the following definitions:[12]

> *Theology* refers to "pure theology," the eternal life of God within himself (*ad intra*). Thus, theology refers to the mysterious inner life of God that remains inaccessible and incomprehensible.
>
> *Economy* refers to the outworking of God's missions and activities, the life of God in creation (*ad extra*). While still mysterious, economy includes God's expressed life to creatures that can be partially accessible and comprehended (e.g., the incarnation and mission of the Son, and Pentecost and the mission of the Spirit).

---

[12] For more on this language within a dogmatic framework, see Fred Sanders, *The Triune God*, New Studies in Dogmatics (Zondervan, 2016). See also Gilles Emery O.P., *The Trinity: An Introduction to Catholic Doctrine of the Triune God*, trans. Matthew Levering, Thomistic Ressourcement Series 1 (Catholic University of America Press, 2011), 199 and 202. We also explore these two terms in relation to trinitarian theology for pastoral ministry in *Ancient Wisdom for the Care of Souls*.

Our partitive exegesis assumes this theology-economy framework when reading texts about the Son. Partitive exegesis also assumes a two-natured single Son when reading Scriptures about the Son: (1) the eternal Son made flesh; (2) the Son does not divest of his divine nature when becoming human; and (3) the Son, mysteriously, becomes the *theandric* (God-man) person during the incarnation: fully divine, simple, *a se*, immutable, and impassible, and simultaneously fully human besides sin, composite, mutable, and passible.

To read partitively is to read with Nicene pressures. While many have worked from Scripture to Creed, we assume the premise and work from Creed to Scripture. Since Nicene theology is the correct outcome of a canonical and theological reading of Scripture, we may use the Nicene Creed as the correct theological rubric to read the Scriptures. Readers can capably and faithfully situate Christological texts within the Son's entire career if they adhere to Nicene pressures.

By understanding theology-economy distinctions and with Nicene pressures in view, we are better equipped to interpret Scripture. For example, when we read about the Son becoming fatigued, weeping over death, or experiencing hunger, we still assume a Philippians 2, Nicene framework. During these experiences, the Son is not in the eternal or exalted position but in the economy of the incarnation. If we neglect to make this exegetical decision, then we are left to suggest that the Son experiences fatigue in his divine life and that God can become tired. Rather than doing justice to the text, we disrupt the text and the theological presuppositions of the biblical author, rupturing the spiritual benefit gained by faithful exegesis. We must keep Nicene theology in mind to interpret our Bibles correctly.

Beyond dissecting what is proper of the Son's divine or human nature, we must remember that whatever the Gospels say about the

Son cannot always be said of God's eternal life.[13] Otherwise, when we read that Jesus became tired, we can conclude that God becomes fatigued. This is not true! What belongs to the eternal life of God subsists equally in the Father, Son, and Spirit. Thus, because of consubstantiality, what the Son is by nature, so too is the Father *only* in aspects concerning the divine nature. This was a significant contention within the debates of fourth-century Trinitarianism. The *Son* took on flesh and became like humanity in all respects except for sin.

Partitive exegesis, therefore, is a cautionary way of reading Scripture that correlates Christological texts to the Son's entire career. The difficulty emerges when we read the four Gospels and forget to read according to the theology-economy framework. We must situate the Son according to the trifold structure of Philippians 2 and Nicaea. This model of reading uses both the scriptural categories and the Nicene article as the framework for discerning the situation of the Son (eternal, incarnate, exalted) and carefully assigns the properties to the Son appropriate for each situation.[14] Reading without this framework creates biblical confusion and theological disjunction.

The Practice of Reading Nicenely: Examples from the Fathers

Athanasius of Alexandria and Gregory of Nazianzus each offer a prime example of practiced partitive exegesis. Athanasius and

---

[13] Lars Koen, "Partitive Exegesis in Cyril of Alexandria's Commentary on the Gospel According to St. John," *Studia Patristica* 25 (1993): 115–21.

[14] For more on Partitive exegesis, see Shawn J. Wilhite, *Cyril of Alexandria's Christological Exegesis: Explorations of Partitive Exegesis in the Dialogues on the Trinity*, Studia Traditionis Theologiae 70 (Brepols, 2025).

Gregory present a biblical vision that discerns from the Scriptures what is said of the Son by virtue of his divinity, and what is said by virtue of his humanity. To read partitively, you must make judgments about the Christological passages by presupposing a two-nature Christology.

For Athanasius, partitive scriptural exegesis is a mode of reading that accords with the scope of the Scriptures. This model of reading does not apply to some Scripture passages but the entirety of Scripture. Athanasius argued:

> Now the scope and character of Holy Scripture, as we have often said, is this: it contains a double account of the Savior; that He was ever God, and is the Son, being the Father's Word and Radiance and Wisdom; and that afterwards for us He took the flesh of a Virgin, Mary Bearer of God, and was made man. And this scope is to be found through inspired Scripture, as the Lord Himself has said, *search the Scriptures, for they are they which testify of me* [John 5:39].[15]

Athanasius understood John 5:39 and the phrase "search the Scriptures" as an invitation to read the Scriptures Christologically using this partitive reading strategy. The entirety of the Scriptures includes a twofold account of the Son: (1) the Son as he is and

[15] *c. Ar.* 3.29. He also notes the following: "Any one, beginning with these passages and going through the whole of the Scripture upon the interpretation which they suggest, will perceive how in the beginning the Father said to Him, *Let there be light* and *let there be a firmament*, and *Let us make man*; but in the fullness of the ages, *he sent Him into the world, not that He might judge the world, but that the world by Him might be saved*, and *how it is written Behold, the Virgin shall be with child, and shall bring forth a Son, and they shall call his Name Emmanuel, which, being interpreted, is God with us.*"

(2) the Son become flesh. This is the basic distinction between theology and economy.

Athanasius offers a better way to understand the Scriptures: We must "recognize what is proper to each."[16] The Scriptures speak in a twofold way about the Son.

> These points we have found it necessary first to examine, that, when we see him doing or saying anything divinely through the instrument of His own body, we may know that He so works, being God, and also, if we see Him speaking or suffering humanly, we may not be ignorant that He bore flesh and became man, and hence He so acts and so speaks. For if we recognize what is proper to each and see and understand that both these things and those are done by one, we are right in our faith and never stray.[17]

Thus, we ought to avoid univocal readings and make a twofold distinction between our exegetical patterns and theological language. There are times when we see the Christ performing or speaking *humanly* (proper to his humanity) and *divinely* (proper to his divinity). In each case, we do not assume two sons but use a two-nature Christology to shape our readings of Scripture (not the other way around). Otherwise, we perform a thin reading of Scripture leading to thin application.

---

[16] In his *ep. Serap.*, Athanasius comments on his perceived practice of partitive readings, from the apostles through the Fathers: "This is the character of the faith which we have received form the Apostles through the Father. Anyone who reads the Scripture must examine and judge where it speaks of the divinity of the Word and where it speaks of his human acts, so that we do not fall prey to the same delirium that has befallen the Arians by understand the one when the other is means" (*ep. Serap.* 2.9).

[17] *c. Ar.* 3.35.

For Gregory of Nazianzus, partitive exegesis assumes vertical imagery for the Son and calls the interpreter to a mystical and spiritual ascent. The interpreter must discern what is above, transcending humanity, and what is lowly, among humanity:

> In sum: you must predicate the more sublime expressions of the Godhead, of the nature which transcends bodily experiences, and the lowlier ones of the compound, of him who because of you was emptied, became incarnate and (to use equally valid language) was "made man." Then next he was exalted, in order that you might have done with the earthbound carnality of your opinions and might learn to be nobler, to ascent with the Godhead and not linger on in things visible but rise up to spiritual realities, and that you might know what belongs to his nature and what to God's plan of salvation.[18]

According to John Behr, this line by Nazianzen is the clearest example of partitive reading in the fourth century.[19] Gregory calls us to first determine if a Christological text refers to the transcendent divine nature or to the human nature and "rise up" to these spiritual realities. For Gregory, partitive reading assumes our abilities to see spiritual realities and to ascend to God in our understanding. Partitive exegesis distinguishes the language that applies to the Son between his humanity and his divinity.

---

[18] *Oration* 29.18.

[19] John Behr, *The Nicene Faith*, vol. 2 of *Formation of Christian Theology* (St. Vladimir's Seminary Press, 2004), 349: "This the clearest statement of the principle of partitive exegesis from the fourth century: some things said of Christ pertain to his divine nature, while other things express what he has done for us in the unfolding of God's plan of salvation."

Biblical Connections

Reading Scripture *nicenely* with Nicene pressures is an exercise both in knowledge and devotion. Thus, we concur with R. B. Jamieson and Tyler R. Wittman that the "goal for exegetically investigating the doctrines of the Trinity and Christology is to pursue, prayerfully, a vision of the risen Christ's glory through faith."[20] As in Philippians 2, 1 John 4 exemplifies the manner of the Son reflected in Nicene theology. The apostle John asserts, "This is how you know the Spirit of God: Every spirit that confesses that Jesus Christ has come in the flesh is from God, but every spirit that does not confess Jesus is not from God" (1 John 4:2–3). He continues, confessing, "And we have seen and we testify that the Father has sent his Son as the world's Savior. Whoever confesses that Jesus is the Son of God—God remains in him and he in God" (vv.14–15). The basic building blocks for understanding the Son's career are present in this confession. Karen Jobes concurs: "The incarnation is the heart of Christian epistemology. Consequently, the converse is also true, that anyone who does not acknowledge Jesus as come in flesh is not of God; that is, they have not acquired the true knowledge of God through the revelation of himself in Jesus Christ."[21] Confessing the incarnation of the Son initiates the path to true knowledge and wisdom. That confession also includes the divine work of the Son from the Father in the work of redemption. Jobes continues: "It is not sufficient to believe in the historical Jesus; one must also believe that the man Jesus was the Son of God whom the Father sent to atone for sin."[22]

---

[20] R. B. Jamieson and Tyler R. Wittman, *Biblical Reasoning: Christological and Trinitarian Rules for Exegesis* (Baker Academic, 2022), 6.

[21] Karen H. Jobes, *1, 2, and 3 John*, Zondervan Exegetical Commentary on the New Testament (Zondervan, 2014), 178.

[22] Jobes, 196.

John brings the confession of the Son's humanity and divinity to bear on our lives: "God has given us eternal life, and this life is in his Son. The one who has the Son has life. The one who does not have the Son of God does not have life" (1 John 5:11–12). The hopes of redemption are bound up in the Son made flesh for our sake. Eternal life hangs in the balance based on the full divinity and humanity of the Son. John Stott notes: "God's testimony concerning Jesus is not only that he is the divine-human Christ but that he is also the life-giver. . . . Eternal life is a free gift which God gives to those who believe in his Son."[23] Reading Scripture *nicenely* confirms the testimony of the apostle John and magnifies his pastoral word to the church. The stakes include not only correct scriptural interpretation, though this is vital, but also the souls of God's people, which rest on the proper confession of, adherence to, and hope in the divine and human Son. Without the Nicene conclusion regarding Scripture and its witness, we remain lost in sin and far from the life of God.

Conclusion

Proper reading and interpretation of the Bible with Nicene pressures provides a more enriching experience of exegesis and theological discourse. The creed is for the Bible, and the Bible is the foundation for the creed. While the creed is from fallible men, its source material is the infallible Word. We can certainly identify with the basic sentiment of the old phrase "no creed but the Bible"; however, we are a creedal people, and the logic and application of this statement are fundamentally flawed. Every text has

[23] John R. W. Stott, *The Letters of John: An Introduction and Commentary*, Tyndale New Testament Commentaries 19 (IVP Academic, 1988), 182–83.

an intended interpretative framework—why not assume a standard creedal statement from the beginning of the Bible reading process, especially one that has shaped the church's theology for 1,700 years? For Christians, the Nicene Creed has always been the confession of God's triunity and the Son's divinity and humanity. Developed throughout church history, the theology-economy scheme serves as a framework for scriptural exegesis essential to understanding God's life. Reading the Bible without Creed is a disservice to God's revealed word and poor stewardship of the faith "once for all delivered to the saints" (Jude 3 ESV).

CONCLUSION

The Legacy of Nicaea and Thinking *Nicenely* for Tomorrow

I (Coleman) was at a park one day with my children, enjoying a rare cool afternoon in the summer months in Texas. As the kids were playing and I was enjoying an iced coffee, I heard one of the children in the park begin singing a familiar tune: the timeless theme song for Super Mario Bros. As this boy ran around singing, other kids in the park heard him and began singing it too. Soon, it was a marvelous children's chorus of retro video game glory, as the kids played, pretending to be Mario and Luigi. This experience reminds me of the effect of sound Christian doctrine. When good doctrine (or bad doctrine) is communicated winsomely and perhaps even in song form, it has the effect of "catching on." A catchy tune rests in the soul and activates in the heart when the familiar notes are played again.

We have tapped into those "familiar notes" from the early traditions of the church. We want to hear the vibrato of the Nicene and pro-Nicene chorus and recite the theological notes in harmony. Our primary aim is to help ourselves and the church to think *nicenely*. Modern trinitarian theology and theological method currently maintains a thin, inadequate engagement with Nicene and pro-Nicene theology. Lewis Ayres observes, "[Modern] Trinitarian theology invokes some of the formulae produced within the fourth century but simultaneously argues that the theological methods that produced those formulae are untenable in modernity."[1]

Some modern readers and theologians like what the fathers of Nicaea concluded but disregard how they got there (the pro-Nicene culture of scriptural reasoning). You cannot have one without the other. To think *nicenely* requires the culture of pro-Nicene theology. Thus, we seek to model some of their theological observations, exegetical patterns, philosophical commitments, and concern for the spiritual life. We pursue a *habitus* that fully embodies the spiritual world, the culture of scriptural exegesis, and the Christian theological imagination. As both scholars and disciples, we think it essential to hold fast to "the faith that was once for all delivered to the saints" (Jude 3 ESV).

The fathers of Nicaea did their best to ensure that the "deposit of faith" was both guarded and understood, despite its detractors. This does not mean we must uncritically accept everything from early Christian history. We do not appreciate some of the fathers' strong, perhaps sinful rhetoric toward Arius and those who embraced his ideas. We abhor the violence committed by some of the bishops. We cannot fathom how Constantine became an immediate doctrinal bodyguard at his ascension to emperor. Still, we must remember the fathers' core motivations and keen pastoral spirit at Nicaea during the subsequent fourth-century reflection. Their lives and thought process matter just as much as their conclusions.

---

[1] Lewis Ayres, *Nicaea and its Legacy: An Approach to Fourth-Century Trinitarian Theology* (Oxford University Press, 2004), 386.

The fathers and the theological controversies in the fourth century are uniquely privileged in Christian history; they provide theological grammar for the church that is still used today! The creedal theology of the fourth century, namely as articulated in the Nicene and Niceno-Constantinople Creeds, continues to shape the essential Christian theological frame. John Behr states: "The significance of this era cannot be overstated: the central elements of Christian theology articulated during the fourth century have been, until very recently, the common inheritance of all Christians, of whatever tradition."[2]

The conclusions of Nicaea resonate today. Nicaea (still) matters. We need the biblical insight orchestrated at Nicaea and amplified by its proponents in the fourth century. Whether you recite the Nicene Creed in corporate worship gatherings or not, Nicaea matters. Whether you are young or old, teacher or student, parent or child, pastor or parishioner, Nicene trinitarianism and pro-Nicene theology have already left a mark on your life as a Christian. We believe it should continue to bear much spiritual fruit in your life and in the church. We should consciously engage in the culture of pro-Nicene theology as a theological *habitus.* Regrettably, Nicaea is a tiny blip on the theological radar for many evangelicals, barely registering in our spiritual life. We hope that through this work, pro-Nicene theology and the Nicene Creed will become an active part of your discipleship conversations and in the worshipping life of the evangelical church.

As Christians, regardless of denomination or confessional position, we are all indebted to the fathers of the fourth century, both those present at Nicaea and those who carried their theological

---

[2] John Behr, *The Nicene Faith, The Formation of Christian Theology*, vol. 2 (St Vladimir's Seminary Press, 2004), 1:xv.

conclusions forward. All Christ-followers can find their theological identity in the Nicene Creed. The creed should continue as a rallying cry for the faithful and a core identity marker for the Christian church. The creed bands Christians together across time and space. As Baptists, we are primarily concerned with seeing our tradition thrive spiritually and theologically. We have the tools to do so, and Nicaea gives us the blueprint to continue blossoming in our confessional heritage.

Our era requires more, not less, theological precision in the face of moral challenges. Doctrine enhances rather than diminishes the church's witness. While some Christian communities falter on the essential points of the gospel, Nicaea testifies to the core truths of Christianity, the absence of which leads to severe theological and moral bankruptcy. While Scripture animates the life of the church, the creed further integrates that Scripture into the theological discourse of the church.

We are, first and foremost, a "people of the Book," but the Nicene Creed is the way we faithfully read that Spirit-inspired book. We emphatically affirm with the apostle Paul that "all Scripture is inspired by God and is profitable for teaching, for rebuking, for correcting, for training in righteousness, so that the man of God may be complete, equipped for every good work" (2 Tim 3:16–17). Yet the faithful exposition of the Scripture must be accompanied by the proper theological understanding of that Word. Thus, the church has always had some rule, standard, or creed to discern faithful exposition from unreliable teaching. As we have continuously expressed in this book, abandoning the creed can create exegetical and theological confusion. Pastors and teachers can shepherd and encourage people faithfully and effectively by holding fast to the creed.

In his high-priestly prayer in John 17:6–8, Jesus prayed, "[Father], I have revealed your name to the people you gave me from the world. They were yours, you gave them to me, and they have kept your word. Now they know that everything you have given me is from you, because I have given them the words you gave me. They have received them and have known for certain that I came from you. They have believed that you sent me."

Divine revelation and trinitarian theology are found together in this prayer. May we seek to understand the mystery of God's life and steward those mysteries for the church. In Scripture, we have been given the sacred words from the Father through the Son by the Holy Spirit. In the creed, the church has put the rule of faith for the Christian church into memorable phrases. We hope that we have helped you be a better steward as we await the glorious return of the Son, when our faith will be made sight.

The Nicene Creed is still necessary. With it, we are equipped to minister well to the souls of one another. Without it, we lack the essential guardrails to keep us from veering off the way of life! By reading and applying the creed, we contemplate God with those who have come before us. May we steward the sacred words of God, using the creed as our guide, to ensure a faithful Christian witness to a lost and dying world.

SUGGESTED READING LIST: PRIMARY SOURCES

Athanasius of Alexandria

Letters to Serapion

ET: Mark DelCogliano, Andrew Radde-Gallwitz, and Lewis Ayres, trans. *Athanasius the Great and Didymus the Blind: Works on the Spirit.* Popular Patristics Series 43. St. Vladimir's Seminary Press, 2011.

A Defense of the Nicene Definition (de Decretis)

ET: Khaled Anatolios. *Athanasius.* The Early Church Fathers. Routledge, 2004.

Basil of Caesarea

On the Holy Spirit

ET: Stephen M. Hildebrand, trans. *St. Basil the Great: On the Holy Spirit.* Popular Patristics Series 42. St. Vladimir's Seminary Press, 2011.

Against Eunomius

ET: Mark DelCogliano and Andrew Radde-Gallwitz, trans. *St. Basil of Caesarea: Against Eunomius.* The Fathers of the Church 122. Catholic University of America Press, 2011.

Gregory of Nazianzus

Theological Orations (or. 28–32)

ET: Frederick Williams and Lionel Wickham, trans. *St Gregory of Nazianzus On God and Christ: The Five Theological Orations and Two Letters to Cledonius.* Popular Patristics Series 23. St Vladimir's Seminary Press, 2002.

Gregory of Nyssa

Against Eunomius

ET: Miguel Brugarolas, ed. *Gregory of Nyssa:* Contra Eunomium *I: An English Translation with Supporting Studies.* Supplements to Vigiliae Christianae 148. Brill, 2018.

Lenka Karfíková, Scot Douglass, and Johannes Zachhuber, eds. *Gregory of Nyssa:* Contra Eunomium *II: An English Version with Supporting Studies.* Supplements to Vigiliae Christianae 82. Brill, 2004.

Johan Leemans and Matthieu Cassin, eds. *Gregory of Nyssa:* Contra Eunomium *III: An English Translation with Commentary and Supporting Studies.* Supplements to Vigiliae Christianae 124. Brill, 2010.

Catechetical Orations

ET: Green, Ignatius, trans. *St Gregory of Nyssa: Catechetical Discourse: A Handbook for Catechists.* Popular Patristics Series 60. St Vladimir's Seminary Press, 2019.

Rufinus of Aquileia

On the Apostles' Creed

ET: J. N. D. Kelly, trans. *Rufinus: A Commentary on the Apostles' Creed.* Ancient Christian Writers 20. Newman, 1955.

SUGGESTED READING LIST: SECONDARY SOURCES

Anatolios, Khaled. *Retrieving Nicaea: The Development and Meaning of Trinitarian Doctrine*. Baker Academic, 2011.

Ayres, Lewis. *Augustine and the Trinity*. Cambridge University Press, 2010.

Ayres, Lewis. *Nicaea and Its Legacy: An Approach to Fourth-Century Trinitarian Theology*. Oxford University Press, 2004.

Barnes, Michel René. *Augustine and Nicene Theology: Essays on Augustine and the Latin Argument for Nicaea*. Cascade Books, 2023.

Behr, John. *The Nicene Faith*. Vol. 1. Formation of Christian Theology. St. Vladimir's Seminary Press, 2004.

Behr, John. *The Nicene Faith*. Vol. 2. Formation of Christian Theology. St. Vladimir's Seminary Press, 2004.

Behr, John. *The Way to Nicaea*. Vol. 1. Formation of Christian Theology. St. Vladimir's Seminary Press, 2001.

Cary, Phillip. *The Nicene Creed: An Introduction*. Lexham, 2023.

DelCogliano, Mark. "Creed of the Council of Constantinople (381)." In *God*, edited by Andrew Radde-Gallwitz, 1:268–69. The Cambridge Edition of Early Christian Writings. Cambridge University Press, 2017.

DelCogliano, Mark. "Creed of the Council of Nicaea (325)." In *God*, edited by Andrew Radde-Gallwitz, 1:114–15. The Cambridge Edition of Early Christian Writings. Cambridge University Press, 2017.

Kim, Young Richard, ed. *The Cambridge Companion to the Council of Nicaea*. Cambridge Companions to Religion. Cambridge University Press, 2021.

Ford, Coleman M. "Salvation in the Patristic Era." In *Historical Theology for the Church*, edited by Jason G. Duesing and Nathan A. Finn, 89–113. B&H Academic, 2021.

Ford, Coleman M., and Shawn J. Wilhite. *Ancient Wisdom for the Care of Souls: Learning the Art of Pastoral Ministry from the Church Fathers*. Crossway, 2024.

Hughes, Amy Brown, and Shawn J. Wilhite. "The Beginnings of a Pro-Nicene Trinitarian Vision: Athanasius of Alexandria on the Activity of the Son and the Spirit." In *On Classical Trinitarianism: Retrieving the Nicene Doctrine of the Triune God*, edited by Matthew Barrett, 38–53. IVP Academic, 2024.

Ortiz, Jared, and Daniel A. Keating. *The Nicene Creed: A Scriptural, Historical & Theological Commentary*. Baker Academic, 2024.

Wilhite, Shawn J. *Cyril of Alexandria's Christological Exegesis: Explorations of Partitive Exegesis in the Dialogues on the Trinity*. Studia Traditionis Theologiae 70. Brepols, 2026.

Wilhite, Shawn J. "What Does It Mean to Be 'Pro-Nicene'? The Development of Pro-Nicene Theology." *Credo Magazine* 10, no. 4 (2020).

GENERAL INDEX

B

C

O

P

R

S

T

V

W

X

SCRIPTURE INDEX